Science, Psychoanalysis, and the Brain

Science, Psychoanalysis, and the Brain is an invitation to a space for dialogue where reflections on neurophysiology are expressed with and guided by depth psychology in mind; a space where neurophysiology resumes its traditional humbled stance toward matters of the psyche, and where the intellectual autonomy of depth psychology is acknowledged. The author leads the reader through the terrain of methodological errors that have plagued recent reductive approaches, paving the way for a dialogue that is based on an alternative, relational approach. Neurophysiology is discussed at a high level of abstraction, enabling genuine analysis of the organization of the brain through its relational interactions with the world.

In this dialogue, where psychology provides a theoretical framework that contributes to physiology, both parties benefit. Neurophysiology gains important constraints and guidance in phrasing meaningful questions, psychology gains further motivation to crystallize its multifaceted concepts. Both disciplines enrich the spectrum of metaphors available to them within their own discourses.

Shimon Marom is a Professor and Head of Physiology at the Faculty of Medicine, Technion – Israel Institute of Technology.

Science, Psychoanalysis, and the Brain

SPACE FOR DIALOGUE

Shimon Marom

Technion – Israel Institute of Technology

CAMBRIDGE
UNIVERSITY PRESS

CAMBRIDGE
UNIVERSITY PRESS

32 Avenue of the Americas, New York, NY 10013-2473, USA

Cambridge University Press is part of the University of Cambridge.

It furthers the University's mission by disseminating knowledge in the pursuit of education, learning, and research at the highest international levels of excellence.

www.cambridge.org
Information on this title: www.cambridge.org/9781107101180

First published 2015

A catalog record for this publication is available from the British Library.

Library of Congress Cataloging in Publication Data
Marom, Shimon, 1958–
Science, psychoanalysis, and the brain : space for dialogue / Shimon Marom.
pages cm
Includes bibliographical references and index.
ISBN 978-1-107-10118-0 (hardback)
1. Psychoanalysis. 2. Psychoanalysis – Physiological aspects. 3. Psychobiology.
4. Psychophysiology. I. Title.
BF175.M28348 2015
150.19′5–dc23 2014043440

ISBN 978-1-107-10118-0 Hardback

To Adi, *by way of a long letter.*

For a hundred and fifty years past the progress of science has seemed to mean the enlargement of the material universe and the diminution of man's importance.... The romantic spontaneity and courage are gone, the vision is materialistic and depressing. Ideals appear as inert by-products of physiology; what is higher is explained by what is lower and treated forever as a case of "nothing but" – nothing but something else of a quite inferior sort.

William James, *Pragmatism*, 1907

Contents

Preface and Acknowledgments

This essay began as a letter to an experienced clinical psychologist, dynamically oriented by education, training, and practice. Out of a developing sense of unease with the nature of the present dialogue between brain science and psychology, she sought understanding, not so much of this or that recent biological finding, but of the roots that feed the stance of neurophysiology toward depth psychology.[1] While meandering in the chasm between physiology and psychology, contemplating the recent history of possible-impossible relations, the letter evolved into the essay offered here: an invitation, issued by a practicing physiologist, intended for dynamically oriented theory-sensitive psychologists and physiologists. It became an invitation to a space where reflections on neurophysiology are expressed and guided by depth psychology in mind; a space where neurophysiology resumes its traditional, humbled attitude toward matters of the psyche, and where the intellectual autonomy of depth psychology is acknowledged. The underlying assumption is that in the basic sense, as opposed to the applied science sense, the meaning

1 Note on terminology: The terms "depth psychology," "psychoanalysis," "psychoanalytic," "psychodynamics," and "dynamic psychology" are used interchangeably to indicate the theory and concepts that have emerged from the various schools of the psychoanalytic movement. These terms are not used here to indicate the practical and technical aspects of the theory and its concepts in the context of therapy. The terms "physiology," "neurophysiology," "brain science," and "neuroscience" are used here to designate any behaviorally relevant physiological system analysis in general, and neural systems in particular.

of neurophysiological and neuroanatomical observables resides in their interpretation in light of psychological theories. A dialogue based on such terms, where psychology provides a theoretical framework that contributes to physiology, is beneficial to both parties: Neurophysiology gains something that is currently wanted – constraints and guidelines in phrasing meaningful questions. Psychology might gain further motivation to crystallize its multifaceted concepts. At all events, both camps might enrich the spectrum of metaphors available to them within their own disciplinary realms.

In Chapter 1 the stage is set with the 1909 Freud-James meeting in America as a soft, literary move that leads to a definition of the objectives of the essay. Chapters 2 and 3 are dedicated to explaining scientific constraints on the choices that may or should be made by a physiologist who contemplates borrowing observables and theoretical constructs from psychology in general, and from depth psychology in particular. Here space is taken to review the state of the art in my own field, neurophysiology, as well as critically to analyze naive mapping of depth psychology concepts to brain activity. To that end, lessons from well-studied relations between levels of organization in physics and in the life sciences are explained, demonstrated, and generalized (with limits) to the relation between psychology and neurophysiology. These analyses show that – contrary to the *zeitgeist* – the former constrains and guides the latter in phrasing meaningful questions. With the above foundations in place, Chapter 4 outlines the elements of depth psychology chosen to negotiate with: the organization of experience as a personal historical process, expressed in terms of relational psychological objects, their development, and their multiple relations with each other and with a dynamic environment populated by interacting others that house their own relational psychological objects. Psychological texts on relational dynamics of objects are read with a physiologist's eye, searching for primitives that transcend differences between psychoanalytical schools, presenting them in a manner that promotes interpretation into the realm of neurophysiology and neuroanatomy. While the choice of relational psychological objects to dialogue with reflects a personal preference, it does seem to have a natural appeal for the neurophysiologist. It resonates with the study of development and dynamics of neural representations, probably the most extensive research topic in neurophysiology, and a theme that has historical roots that are shared by both fields. But, more important from the point of view of neurophysiological research: what psychologists are telling us on the relational nature of objects has consequences on how we – neurophysiologists – should phrase and approach our research objectives, and how far we can take our interpretations of physiological observables that are (by definition) limited to processes that take place within the individual.

The longest chapter of the essay, Chapter 5, is an embodiment of the dialogue. It describes neuroanatomy and neurophysiology in light of the primitives of relational dynamics in psychology. It is an attempt to analyze different ways to approach neurophysiology given the facts of depth psychology. Physiology and neuroanatomy are presented at a rather abstract level, thus making space for a dialogue between the two languages. Effort is made to present things in a way that enables both the psychologically educated reader and the well-informed neurophysiologist to remain engaged. The somewhat old construct of a Conceptual Nervous System is reintroduced, and serves in the analysis of development and dynamics of physiological objects. Physiological concepts are offered and developed (internal space, discontent, symmetry breaking, inter-object interaction, and adaptation) that reflect aspects of the psychological theory. A need for a form of relational physiology is voiced, echoing the Rashevsky-Rosen school of relational biology, focusing on the organization of coupled systems beyond material realization. The chapter brings arguments from the fields of evolution, psychology, neurophysiology, and anatomy, making use of texts from the history shared by both fields. Reading these old texts was an exercise in modesty; each and every time the peregrinations in the chasm between psychology and physiology seemed to bring me closer to an original idea – a small oasis of my own – I found it already colonized and cultivated by the founders of our disciplines. The chapter ends with pointing at the challenge entailed by a relational approach to neurophysiological research. Chapter 6 closes the essay with a touch of romanticism and politics of ideology.

A few more words might help in positioning this essay with reference to other points of view. The text is not an account of mind-brain philosophy, or philosophy of psychoanalysis or language in this context; these are available in many books published over the past century by eminent, more suitable, writers. A conscious decision was made to shy away from formal philosophical and metaphysical arenas. Instead, the focus is on how things look from the stance of a practicing scientist, reflecting a personal take; expressing appreciation of the need for a theoretical input from psychology, a position formed over years of physiological analysis of dynamics and function in large-scale neural networks. No claim is made that the approach and ideas expressed in this text represent the mainstream of practicing neurophysiologists, although they might represent many (albeit silent, public-relations-wise) of us.

The issue of reductionism, a loosely defined and often overloaded term, is central in discussions that concern relations between psychology and the sciences. The text is critical about naive mixing of scales in general, and about naive mapping of psychological concepts to this or that brain activity in particular. But it would be a mistake to read the essay as a critique on *any* attempt to map across constructs at different scales; the most beautiful intellectual insights are due to such mappings. Much may be gained by allowing for exchange of ideas between fields of knowledge – regardless of the scales involved – as long as the uniqueness of each field is respected. There are means to do this properly, and they usually involve abstractions of the kind offered in the present text.

The point of view presented in an essay of this particular kind inevitably reflects the idiosyncratic set of texts with which the writer is surrounded and consults. Several of the authors of these texts I feel particularly obliged to mention: Robert Rosen for *Life Itself* (1991), a tour in the basement floor of the sciences, where Nicolas Rashevsky's concept of relational biology is presented, as well as the treasure of humbled appreciation for the limits and consequences of our scientific abstractions and formalisms. Gerald M. Edelman, whose book *Neural Darwinism* (1987) exposes the making of neurophysiology in the wider context of the life sciences, rather than treating the brain as a substance different from all other living matter. Walter M. Elsasser who, in his *Reflections on a Theory of Organisms* (1987), offers a glimpse into the profound complexity of biology and points to a good enough way to handle it, scientifically. Henry Atlan, a biophysicist and philosopher whose book *Enlightenment to Enlightenment: Intercritique of Science and Myth* (*A tort et à raison*, 1986) describes the possibility of establishing a dialogue between the sciences and the humanities. Marguerite Yourcenar for *The Abyss* (*L'Oeuver au Noir*, 1968), the story of Zeno of Bruges and the protracted delivery of modern human thought, told and analyzed in the most profound way imaginable. Richard C. Lewontin's essays on biology and genetics, particularly his *Biology as Ideology* (1991), which resonates with my personal biases and never fails to impress in their intellectual integrity and their sensitivity to the present state of biological art in the wider historical, social, and political contexts. Percy W. Bridgman's *The Logic of Modern Physics* (1927) for his analysis of our limitations in interpreting "objective" findings and the manners by which the method of measurement can be improved to handle these limitations, to an extent. Valentino Braitenberg, whom I had the honor of meeting, for his ability to abstract the complexity of the matters at hand. Braitenberg's *On the Texture of Brains* (1973) is a beautiful exposition of (using his words) "neuroanatomy as a kind of psychology." Philip

W. Anderson for his two papers on the concept of *More Is Different* (1972 and 2001). And Denis Noble, whose work on the physiology of excitability is widely acknowledged, for *The Music of Life* (2006), a clear polemic exposition of the difficulties and challenges faced by the current structural, reductive approaches to the life sciences, and for his insistence on carrying with pride and dignity the ensigns of physiology. John Eccles for his *Evolution of the Brain: Creation of the Self* (1989), an analysis of the history of our kind, leading to the writings of Phillip V. Tobias and more recent scholars who study paleoanthropology. Jacques Barzun for the depth of *A Stroll with William James* (1983). Robert D. Richardson for his encyclopedic description of the life of *William James: In the Maelstrom of American Modernism* (2006). Saul Rosenzweig for *Freud, Jung and Hall the King-Maker* (1992), an emphatic, touching description of the settings that surrounded Freud's journey to America in 1909. John C. Flugel, whose book *A Hundred Years of Psychology* (1934) I encountered by chance in an old bookshop somewhere in Galilee, a panoramic view of the history of a discipline as conceived by a scholar in the beginning of the twentieth century. As for the visit to the terrain of psychological objects, I am infinitely obliged from afar to Thomas H. Ogden. His texts, in particular his paper on "The Concept of Internal Object Relations" (1983), the book that followed (*The Matrix of the Mind* [1986]), and his more recent *Creative Readings* (2012), opened for me a window to a whole world of Object Relations theorists and their writings. And, of course, the writings, and more so the images, of the two heroes, James and Freud, whom we secretly and humbly follow from behind, listening to a dialogue they have never had a chance to complete.

Acknowledgments. I thank my colleagues and students at Technion's Network Biology Laboratory, as well as the editors and reviewers at Cambridge University Press, for their candid and important comments on earlier versions of the text. I am especially grateful to Daniel Dagan, Erez Braun, Asaf Gal, Ron Meir, and Noam Ziv for encouragement and precious discussions throughout the writing phase. Within the closer perimeter, I am beholden – first and foremost – to Adi for her love, inspiration, and teachings; to my son Nimrod for his support, invaluable advice, and delicate reviews throughout my negotiations with this subject matter; to my son Omer who patiently and emphatically stood beside me, enabling the space and time required. And to the memory of David Melamed, whom I never met, for the treasures he entrusted to me.

1 A Lost Dialogue

A dialogue between two men took place early September 1909 in Worcester, New England. One of the two was William James, 67 years old, physiologist, medical doctor, psychologist, and philosopher. A portrait of James from around that time reveals a slender man with good posture, warm yet penetrating eyes, and a wild grayish beard. Being an empiricist in the most fundamental sense possible, James insisted on experiencing all, shying away from nothing, the simplest or the apparently bizarre, exploring for "irreducible and stubborn facts."[1] Robert Richardson, the author of James's extensive biography, says that "consistency, for James, was not in itself a virtue. Vacillation was ... a fixed habit. He was so open to almost any kind of experience that he was apt to change his mind repeatedly about any single piece of it, from a career plan to a recent book."[2] James was the author of many psychology texts, the most celebrated of which is the 1890 *Principles of Psychology*; while not the first textbook of the discipline (textbooks by, for example, Bain and Spencer had been published earlier), James's *Principles* remains the most relevant to date. It is a systematic analysis of a wide array of human behaviors, ranging from such basic concepts as Habits, Instincts, and Perception to complex phenomena such as Association, Thought, Consciousness of Self, Emotions, and Hypnotism. James's contributions to philosophy

1 Richardson (2007, pp. 5 and 297).
2 Ibid., p. 152.

are of utmost importance, largely due to their emphasis on the psychological machineries underlying key philosophical concepts. He was a firm believer in (and one of the founders of) *Pragmatism*, a conceptual framework much abused over the years, which to James was no less than the path towards knowing what is true by means of ongoing negotiations with the observed, tightly connected to relational dynamics and depth psychology, as will become evident in later chapters of this essay. "By their fruits ye shall know them, not by their roots"[3] was one of James's favorite aphorisms, variants of which appear in multiple places throughout his writings.

The other man was Sigmund Freud. In September 1909, as testified by several photographs taken in Worcester, Freud (at the age of 53) seems almost as old as James, having a somewhat embittered look, with an all-white, well-cultivated beard, slightly bent forward and holding a stylish walking stick. At that time Freud's ideas, already known in the world of academic psychology, were much criticized but influential. He was called to Worcester by Stanley Hall, the president of Clark University, himself an eminent American psychologist and educator, an old friend, and often contender, of James. Stanley Hall invited Freud to present his theoretical framework to the Americans in a series of lectures as part of a conference in honor of the twentieth anniversary of the university. Freud had hesitated, but eventually accepted the invitation and sailed to Worcester from Europe, embarking from Bremen on board the *Norddeutscher Lloyd* ship *George Washington* on August 21.[4] He travelled with two of his apostles – Carl Jung of Zurich (who had been invited independently of Freud)[5] and Sandor Ferenczi of Budapest – a journey in which much is said to have happened

[3] James (1902, p. 26); adapted from Matthew 7:20 (KJV) "Wherefore by their fruits ye shall know them."

[4] Jones (1955, p. 54).

[5] While Jung said so, and likewise insisted in his biography, there is no indication to that effect in correspondence with Hall. See Rosenzweig (1992, footnote 2 in pp. 355–6).

between Freud and Jung, maybe the beginning of the collapse of their relationship. They arrived in New York City on August 30, spending several days there, and then took the train to Worcester.

The atmosphere in American academic psychology and its relation to the European (largely German) school around the time of Freud's arrival at Clark University, is described aptly by Flugel in his 1934 book on the history of psychology:

> [T]he rapid rise of American psychology is beyond all doubt one of the most striking scientific events of the last two decades of the nineteenth century.... But in taking over psychology, America distinctly modified the German attitude. From the very first the principal features of this modification were clearly apparent. They can be summarized very briefly under three heads: (1) a much greater interest in the genetic standpoint; (2) a distrust of introspection and (3) an emphasis on individual differences rather than on the general characteristics of the human mind.[6]

These are the seeds of biologism, behaviorism, and the dominance of quantitative mental tests in America throughout the twentieth century.

Freud and Jung stayed at President Hall's house during the one-week conference. William James arrived at Worcester toward the end of the conference, on the evening of Thursday, September 9, "in order to see what Freud was like."[7] In itself, James's attendance was a valuable statement of an intention, by one of the most distinguished American intellectuals, to understand the principles underlying the psychoanalytical movement. He stayed the night in Hall's house, together with Freud and Jung, and planned to take the next day's (Friday) evening train back home to Boston.

It is reasonable to assume that Freud was eager to impress James; maybe this drove him to change the subject of his planned Friday

[6] Flugel (1934, pp. 210–11).
[7] A letter to Theodore Flournoy, September 28, 1909. In *The Letters of William James* (1920), vol. II.

lecture,[8] practically repeating large portions of his previous day's lecture on dreams, slips of the tongue, and accidental behavior, conveying the message that interpretation of dreams and accidental acts are "the *Via Regia* to the knowledge of the unconscious."[9] Freud asserted that his most regular observation thus made is that the symptoms of his patients are traceable back to impressions from their early sexual life. "In all cases," he said, a thorough explanation of present symptoms "finds its way back to the time of puberty and early childhood.... [it] is the enduring, repressed wishes of childhood which provide the power for the formation of symptoms ... [T]hese powerful childhood wishes are almost invariably of a sexual nature."[10] James was there, listening to Freud's message to an allegedly prudish American audience.[11]

It was probably difficult for Freud and James to have time alone during the twenty-four hours of James's visit. Therefore, Freud, by invitation, joined James on Friday evening on his one-and-a-half mile walk from Hall's house to Worcester railway station, where they would go their separate ways, never to see each other again: James died in 1910. The failure of the genuine attempt made by these two great men to understand each other within the limited space and time (one-and-a-half miles, maybe one hour), was literally heartbreaking:[12] "He [James] stopped suddenly, handed me a bag he was carrying and asked me to walk on, saying that he would catch me up as soon as he had got through an attack of angina pectoris which was just coming on." James did see some possible merit in Freud's

8 Rosenzweig (1992, pp. 171–2).
9 Ibid., p. 418.
10 Ibid., p. 426.
11 In a letter to Jung, while contemplating the option of accepting the invitation to come to America (McGuire, 1974, pp. 195–7), Freud expressed his concerns that "once they discover the sexual core of our psychological theories they will drop us. Their prudery and their material dependence on the public are too great."
12 Freud (1925, p. 52).

idea; in a letter to one of his colleagues he expressed hopes that Freud and his disciples "will push their ideas to their utmost limits, so that we may learn what they are. They can't fail to throw light on human nature; but I confess that he made on me personally the impression of a man obsessed with fixed ideas. I can make nothing in my own case with his dream theories, and obviously 'symbolism' is a most dangerous method."[13] In another letter he writes: "I strongly suspect Freud, with his dream-theory, of being a regular *hallucinê*."[14] These are difficult words to read, even today, especially when streaming from a pen belonging to a man of such depth and openness as James. Strangely, Freud (an otherwise obsessive note keeper) never commented, at least not in writing – as far as I can tell – on what James had said (or did not say) to him in this walk to the station. It is strange, because no one single person throughout the American academic world was more strongly identified with the underpinnings of psychology than James at that time. All we know is that Freud came back to Europe with a feeling that "America is a mistake; a gigantic mistake, it is true, but none the less a mistake,"[15] complaining of the traumatic impacts of the trip on his gastrointestinal system and – quite bizarrely – that his "handwriting has deteriorated so very much since the American trip."[16] Nothing on the intellectual interaction with James, whose scientific approbation Freud surely sought.

The failure to interact with each other, to initiate a genuine dialogue between the then budding Freudian theory that strived for scientific backing, and the age-old, systematic, seemingly solid thread from anatomy to physiology to psychology to mind and philosophy,

[13] A letter to Theodore Flournoy, September 28, 1909. In *The Letters of William James*, vol. II.

[14] A letter to Mary Calkins (September 19, 1909), in Rosenzweig (1992, p. 174).

[15] Jones (1955, p. 60). The Jones account of Freud's ambiguity towards the American experience is educative and humorous (pp. 53–60).

[16] Letter from Sigmund Freud to Ernest Jones, January 27, 1910, in *The Complete Correspondence of Sigmund Freud and Ernest Jones 1908–39*, pp. 42–3.

a thread to which James devoted his intellectual life, should not have come as a surprise. It is James who wrote of scientists yielding "to the pleasure of taking for true what they happen so vividly to conceive as possible … [representing] a mood of Faith, not Science."[17] It is James, rooted in physiology, who stated that "the ignoring of data is, in fact, the easiest and most popular mode of obtaining unity in one's thought,"[18] and that the "theorizing mind tends always towards the oversimplification of its materials."[19] While James rejected "the assertion … that the only sound psychological science is that founded in physiology" and against "the most brutal materialism,"[20] he clearly articulated his faith that "the way to a deeper understanding of the order of our ideas lies in the direction of cerebral physiology.… [I]t is only as incorporated in the brain that such schematism can represent anything *causal*."[21] The dialogue between James and Freud was a dialogue between one who was open to explore any direction, yet restrained by his insistence on "irreducible and stubborn facts," and one who was significantly more relaxed regarding facts, but insisted on seeing things through his own prism – psychoanalysis, as he envisioned it.

Depth psychology and physiology went their separate ways. The psychoanalytic movement, arguably the only branch of psychology that dares to hypothesize on the dynamics of motives and conflicts underlying human psychic life, distanced itself from issues of matter, focusing on the development of a rich conceptual framework, addressing psychodynamics independently of the underlying physical machinery. This separation process stands in sharp contrast to the development of other branches of psychology that took less insecure paths, attending to aspects of human behavior to which the

17 Richardson (2007, p. 163).
18 Ibid., p. 184.
19 James (1902, p. 32).
20 Richardson (2007, p. 195).
21 James (1950[1890], volume 1, p. 593).

method of measurement might be applied. These other branches of scientific psychology (for instance, the study of perception, learning, memory, categorization, and decision making) position themselves at a more convenient place in their negotiations with the discipline of physiology. Moreover, they make every possible effort to distinguish themselves from the misty language of psychodynamics. At the same time, physiology had confined itself, until very recently, to matter, with marginal reference to the mind. A dialogue between physiology and psychology, where realized, was limited to the above-mentioned branches of scientific psychology that focus on measurable behavior. Only in one (critical) front – the borderline of medical practice – did clashes flare here and there between applied physiology and the psychoanalytic movement; most notable is the Osheroff versus Chestnut Lodge case.[22] These clashes, however, were immediately extinguished, usually by psychoanalysts clearing the way and withdrawing from the field of conflict.

Over the past decade or two we have been witnessing a change in the relations between depth psychology and physiology. Technological advancements in manipulating and measuring brain activities around the transition from the twentieth into the twenty-first century, taken together with an atmosphere that rewards interdisciplinary approaches, have brought neurophysiology and psychoanalysis into contact again. Ernst Mach (1838–1916) referred to such often seen transient phenomena, where fields that have developed in parallel come into contact, hoping that relating them to each other might throw light on otherwise hidden important facts. On such occasions there is a natural tendency to think that one of the fields may be absorbed by the other. But, says Mach:

> [T]he period of buoyant hope, the period of over-estimation of this relation which is supposed to explain everything, is quickly followed

22 Klerman (1990, 1991); Stone (1990).

by a period of disillusionment, when the two fields in question are once more separated, and each pursues its own aims, putting its own special questions and applying its own peculiar methods. But on both of them the temporary contact leaves abiding traces behind.... [T]he temporary relation between them brings about a transformation of our conceptions, clarifying them and permitting of their application over a wider field than that for which they were originally formed."[23]

Regarding the matter in hand, whichever direction of abiding traces one seeks to identify – psychoanalysis to neurophysiology or vice versa – one must be aware of the danger of making the category errors that are entailed in the mixing of scales and levels of organization, inherent to wandering within the psycho-physiological chasm. Scientists tend to become less sensitive to such category errors – otherwise unacceptable within established scientific disciplines – when jumping scales across disciplines; more so when it comes to making statements about psychology, the "permitted" discipline.

With Ernst Mach's perceptive comment in mind, a potentially important project – beyond the scope of the present essay – might be imagined, where psychologists attempt to identify abiding traces of transformations within psychoanalysis, brought about by modern approaches to complexity and organization in dynamical systems theory,[24] or by neurophysiological findings.[25]

But this essay is about the complementary direction: identification of traces of those transformations that depth psychology imposes on neurophysiology, transformations that survive the disillusionment with relations that are supposed to explain everything. To this end, the century-old dialogue between physiology and depth psychology is presented in a manner that might help in defining what can and, more important, what cannot be exchanged between

23 Mach (1914[1897], p. 83).
24 See, for instance, Stolorow (1997).
25 Kandel (1998, 1999).

the two disciplines. Acknowledging the inherent irreducibility of the depth psychology discourse, the dialogue – as presented here – departs from the aura of physiological chauvinism that dominates at the present time. It is important to do so in order to protect physiology from an ignominious materialism when it comes to issues of psychic processes. It is vital – for the benefit of neurophysiology – to secure the intellectual autonomy of depth psychology discourse from the impacts of a naive reductionism that aims to explain away psychic concepts by pointing at biological mechanisms and semantically empty causal relations.

While I subscribe to the belief that no direct mapping between the concepts that constitute psychoanalytic and neurophysiological discourses is available for us *in principle*, proper abstraction may expose domains within each of the disciplines, through which a meaningful dialogue may be reified. After all, both disciplines share a history of intellectual interest in relational, functional development and adaptation of representations over extended spatial and temporal scales; they share a history of intellectual interest in the ways representations (of admittedly very different kinds of objects) are formed, grow, interact, split, and merge; they share a history of confusion about what is pre-determined and what is open to evolve over the human life cycle; what is physical and tangible, and what is independent of structure. Taken together with the links between them, these and related issues constitute a space for dialogue; a floor where a genuine attempt may be made by both depth psychology and neurophysiology to understand each other and – importantly – to define the boundaries of their trades, their individuation. In this process, neurophysiology is a major donee by possible gain of meaning.

The present invitation to establish a deferential dialogue between depth psychology and physiology is mainly intended for the sake of physiology. It is in itself an unvoiced dialogue that might have taken place within the minds of physiologists that are interested in meaningful input from depth psychology, but are concerned by the simplistic biologism that characterizes several of the recent trends. The dialogue is presented as a collection of thoughts, associations, and reflections that critically examine potential points of contact in an abstract space between the two disciplines. Concepts are phrased in terms that promote a dialogue, focusing on generic aspects of depth psychology and neurophysiology, primitives that are situated at the basis of these fields. In the analysis of neural structures and dynamics no specific brain anatomical loci are mentioned, nor cellular or genetic correlates of behavior. Not in order to spare the psychologists the agony of sinking into physiological technicalities do I refrain from localizing functions in the brain. Rather, it is because localization in its broader sense is the very thing that is detrimental to a dialogue between depth psychology and physiology.

We carry with us the symptoms and signs of the James-Freud 1909 symbolic failure to converse, sometimes paradoxically twisted, but clear to the eyes of those who seek them. Maybe it is time now to resume deferential tones dissolved too early, to dialogue in a more suitable space and definitely with no intentions in mind, nor in its matter, either to condescend or to ignore each other for one more century.

2 Scales and Constraints

Reflecting on explanations for an observed macroscopic phenomenon, most of us seamlessly take the reductionist's path. The idea of an explanation would involve – in one way or another – what may be called the funnel view. This is the assertion that, while at the macroscopic level things seem mysterious, as one goes down the physical scales to observe smaller and smaller spatial or temporal elements of the phenomenon, one expects matters to become clearer. Moreover, the macroscopic mystery – according to this conviction – is an aggregation of simple, or at least simple-to-define, spatial or temporal microscopic objects. In this envisioned hierarchical structure, which extends from the microscopic-simple to macroscopic-complex, the latter is constrained by the former: every model or theory pertaining to a given scale must conform to the constraints imposed by the smaller scales below. This linear daisy chain gives rise to a well-formed structure, the bedrock of self-confidence characterizing the natural sciences.

While the reality experienced by practicing scientists is far from the idealized funnel view, one cannot overemphasize the power of developing theories that are constrained from below. The very attempt to constrain a macroscopic theory by microscopic considerations is an invaluable drive in the process of constructing a conceptual framework. Being constrained does not mean that every microscopic detail should be taken into account; good science is based on the art of judging what should (can) and what should not (cannot) be taken from below. And even more importantly, as will shortly be explained, being constrained from below does not mean intellectual subservience.

Freud, of course, understood the importance of microscopic constraints for the development of a solid theoretical framework. But his attempt to physiologically constrain psychological concepts failed. He turned back into the sea of unfathomable life, abandoning the 1895 *Project for Scientific Psychology*[1] in favor of a richer, more natural language. It was undeniably wise to do so. The capacity to develop and manipulate psychoanalytic concepts using the Freudian language launched psychology into a fascinating orbit that intersected the intellectual and actual lives of many. This achievement, however, came at a price. It did not take long for hard-nosed science to respond, distancing itself from the "murky" language of psychoanalysis. For almost a century, both psychology and the sciences regarded the position as fair: science does not deal with the subjective, while psychoanalysis remains in the abstract domain, free of any requirement to materialize its concepts. Even if one were willing to accept the possibility that detachment from the sciences might entail a poverty of constraints in the construction of psychological theories, this same detachment enabled psychoanalytic concepts to be enriched without being hindered by science. This is why the field developed so well; it is difficult to imagine concepts such as Klein's "good" and "bad" objects surviving the scrutinizing, rigorous eyes of natural scientists.

An emphatic yet critical reader might admit a sense of inconvenience that attaches to such a blatant divorce of psychoanalysis from the sciences. From physics, upwards through chemistry, biology, physiology, and simple sensory and motor aspects of behavior, there seems to be an intellectual continuum; and then the line is

[1] Freud (1895, pp. 281–391); in November 29, 1895, weeks after the initiation of the project, in a letter to Fliess he writes: "It seems to me to have been a kind of aberration" [Freud (1954, p. 134)].

somehow broken, exactly when it gets to the things that are of most interest – our motivations, conflicts, and unconscious choices in life. Is depth psychology really impermeable to negotiations with science as we are trained to know it? If so, why is it that theories about motivations, conflicts, and unconscious choices in life seem intellectually autonomous from the scientific daisy chain of scales and constraints? Is this state of affairs unique to depth psychology? And, finally, what are the consequences of the intellectual autonomy of psychoanalysis for our attempt to define a space for dialogue?

To answer these questions, two core assumptions of the funnel view are considered: (1) that fundamental microscopic principles and laws are necessary, or (at least) sufficient, in order to understand macroscopic phenomena; and (2) that microscopic objects of analysis are "simpler" in comparison to macroscopic entities. We are led to the conclusion that both assumptions cannot hold. We then contemplate the impacts of this conclusion on the motivation to reduce macroscopic phenomena to their alleged microscopic mechanisms, and the means by which such reduction is attempted – namely, reverse engineering. The status of attempts to link psychoanalytic concepts to biology in general, and neurophysiology in particular, is evaluated. The chapter concludes with a call for an alternative to the funnel view, a form of relations between neurophysiology and psychoanalysis, a dialogue that relies on interpretations and projections between relevant abstracted physiological and psychological concepts, rather than on physiological constraints on psychological phenomena.

More Is Different

The recent history of physics provides an important lesson to both physiologists and psychologists who attempt bridging the gap between different scales or levels of organization. Philip Anderson, an American physicist and Nobel laureate, coined the expression "More Is Different" in 1972.[2] As so vividly told by him in later years,[3] the world of physics was practically dominated in the late 1960s by scientists subscribing to the view that particle (also known as high energy) physics – the physics aimed at identifying the forces governing interactions between the most elementary constituents of the atom and its nucleus – is the only intellectually challenging specialty, attracting the best among young physicists. The academic atmosphere in the 1960s may be appreciated by reading a cluster of celebrated articles published in the March 1965 issue of *Science* magazine: at that time physicists were applying for national-scale budgets in order to build and operate accelerators that could generate enough energy to force collisions between particles and detect the products of these collisions. The purpose of such endeavors was to identify the theoretically predicted (or, better, unpredicted) fundamental elements of nature and to estimate the forces involved in keeping them together. It is undeniably a most challenging and worthy objective, from both the pure intellectual and the applied science points of view.

There are, of course, other kinds of research in physics, involving matters on larger scales; the physics of condensed matter (or, in its earlier expression, solid state physics) from molecules to objects that we actually see around us: water, wood, stones, metals, organisms, and so forth. But the 1965 *Science* articles openly argued that particle physics is more fundamental, in the sense that practically all other kinds of physics, chemistry, and even biology, are phenomena to be explained in terms of laws defined at the level of elementary, microscopic interactions. To quote Victor F. Weisskopf:[4] "Intensive research goes for the fundamental laws, extensive research goes for the explanation of phenomena in terms of known fundamental laws.… Solid

[2] Anderson (1972).
[3] Anderson (2001).
[4] Weisskopf (1965, p. 1552).

state physics, plasma physics and perhaps also biology are extensive. High energy and a good part of nuclear physics are intensive."

Note the distinction between those dealing with phenomena and the ones that "go for" fundamental laws. For readers who are not familiar with the jargon that dominates in certain circles of the sciences: "phenomenologists" are second grade scientists. H.A. Bethe stated blatantly in that *Science* issue: "Solid state theory is still a very fruitful field, giving many important advances and new insights into the working of ... complicated systems. However, one could hardly claim that it advances our *fundamental* understanding of nature."[5] Leaving aside the hubris that characterizes these statements, the overall picture promoted is that particle physics is the science that defines the fundamental laws governing the things we experience in the world, whereas all other kinds of science – from the single molecule to biology – are considered "mere chemistry."[6] In other words, these other sciences are no more than applied versions of the fundamental laws defined by particle physicists, unique case studies that reflect non-generic and less challenging settings.

I assume that those eminent particle physicists did not simply try to manipulate their audience in order to obtain the national-scale funding needed for building huge accelerators; that they were stating what they actually believed – no new fundamental laws or concepts arise as we go up the ladder of organization, from the atom to the molecule to the population of molecules to cells and clusters of cells, to individual organisms and their societies. The elementary laws are there, constituting a "theory of everything" – highly relevant to all scales, determining what we observe, limited only by unique circumstances (special cases) that cannot advance "our fundamental understanding of nature," as Bethe stated. It is astonishing to learn how simplistic eminent scientists can be.

5 Bethe (1965, p. 1551).
6 Anderson (2001).

Many years later, Anderson reflected on the serious consequences of the fundamentalists' view of the world at the time:

> 1967 was a temporary maximum of arrogance among the particle physics establishment, riding high in government advisory circles ... and in possession of funding ... which made their employment profitable for any university. There was for instance difficulty in getting condensed matter colleagues recognized by the National Academy of Sciences, and many physics departments in major universities such as Yale, Columbia, and Princeton had only token representation of the field of condensed matter.[7]

Reading these sentences, it is difficult to avoid contemplating the academic context of (fundamental?) neuroscience and (phenomenological?) psychology.

But things changed, largely due to the success of "phenomenological" physicists who were able to show formally that concepts, entities, and laws characterizing condensed matter *are not* consequences of the laws that govern the individual, microscopic elements below. Consider, for instance, the laws (that is, forms of relations between relevant variables) that are used in order to explain the concepts of fluidity, viscosity, elasticity – none of which has any meaning at the level of a single particle: they exist only at the level of populations of particles and cannot possibly be predicted from the fundamental laws that govern the single particle. Stated more generally: when the scale of a system is changed – from the microscopic to the macroscopic, from a single object (for example, atom, or cell, or organism) to a population of objects (e.g., molecule, organ, or society, respectively) – new laws and concepts emerge that are independent of the actual structures and laws that govern the smaller scales. In fact, the same macroscopic concepts and laws can (and are) realized by many different microscopic principles. Somewhat paradoxically, viewed

[7] Ibid., pp. 1–2.

from this angle, it is the study of the microscopic level that becomes a unique, non-generic instance, a "phenomenological case study" of the more generic understanding of the laws that govern the macroscopic level. This macroscopic higher level, in Anderson's words, enjoys "intellectual autonomy … from the tyranny of the fundamental equations which constitute the [lower level] 'theory of everything' …" that he conceives "… as the theory of almost nothing."[8]

Anderson's More Is Different does not deny the unmatched achievements of small-scale physics. More Is Different points to the intellectual autonomy of the larger from the lesser, thus imposing limits on naive extrapolations in the application of the funnel view. At each level, "entirely new laws, concepts, and generalizations are necessary, requiring inspiration and creativity to just as great a degree as in the previous one. Psychology is not applied biology, nor biology applied chemistry."[9]

Anderson and many other members of the condensed matter community based their statements on a formal understanding of the nature of interactions between two well-defined physical levels of organization within a given discipline. As will be discussed, extrapolations of this formal framework to interactions between other domains (physical or intellectual) are not as well grounded. Nevertheless, they feel right. The main message to us

[8] Ibid., p. 7.

[9] Anderson (1972). Richard Feynman, as evident in one of his *Messenger Lectures* on the character of physical law, reflected along the same line of More Is Different in the general context of hierarchies of ideas, extending to the humanities:

> [A]ll the sciences, and not just the sciences but all the efforts of intellectual kinds, are an endeavour to see the connections of the hierarchies, to connect beauty to history, to connect history to man's psychology, man's psychology to the working of the brain, the brain to the neural impulse, the neural impulse to the chemistry, and so forth, up and down, both ways.… And I do not think either end is nearer to God. To stand at either end, and to walk off that end of the pier only, hoping that out in that direction is the complete understanding, is a mistake. [Feynman (1965), pp. 125–6.]

(physiologists, psychologists) concerns the caution one must exercise when jumping across scales of organization. New fundamental concepts (transference, depression, repression, conflict, psychosis, love, and so forth) might emerge and become meaningful at the psychological level, with no insightful trace of meaning at the microscopic physiological level (gene, protein, synapse, cell, unique brain area). It is true for the science of simple things (physics), a science that focuses on objects that may be contemplated or viewed under well-controlled isolation conditions. It most probably holds for sciences of more complex organizations – biology, psychology, sociology – where the very possibility of isolating an object (system) from its relations with the environment is questionable, even as a *gedankenexperiment*.

The general idea captured by Anderson's More Is Different has surfaced in debates on the relations between physiology to psychology ever since the inception of the latter as a research discipline in Europe. Around the 1900s, when Freud developed and presented his psychoanalytic framework, the psychological academic arena was much influenced by the school of Wilhelm Wundt (1832–1920), probably the first to engage in psychology as an independent academic field. Wundt's concepts, and their implementation in experimental psychology, had an unparalleled impact on the development of psychology. Many of the schools described in later chapters of this essay – European and American – used Wundt's ideas as a reference point, explicitly or implicitly, favorably or less so. Wundt was very clear regarding the matter in hand: psychological theory must be based on, and validated by, psychological investigation, divorced from the facts of physiological "substance." For him, the questions that psychology has to solve:

> … can surely never consist in applying, in connection with psychical processes, principles which do not belong to the psychical side of life. It must much rather consist in the attempt to gain principles

> out of the contents of our psychical life, just as in the reverse case physiological investigation of the change of matter and energy in the organism does not in the least, and rightly so, trouble itself with the psychical qualities of the organism.[10]

Wundt classified psychology with what he called "the mental sciences," along with (for example) history, sociology, philology, law, a mixture of present social sciences, and humanities:

> We only need to cast a glance at the sciences most closely connected with psychology, i.e. the so-called mental sciences, in order to become aware of the emptiness and futility of this psychological conception of "substance." The name "mental science" has only the right to exist, so long as these departments of learning are based upon the facts of psychology – the mental science in the most general sense of the term. Now when would a historian, philologist, or jurist make use of any other means to understand some phenomenon or of any other arguments to prove some statement than those which spring from immediate facts of mental life? Why then should the standpoint of psychology be in absolute contradiction to the standpoints of its most nearly related sciences? Psychology must not only strive to become a useful basis for the other mental sciences, but it must also turn again and again to the historical sciences, in order to obtain an understanding for the more highly developed mental processes.[11]

These clear and unambiguous sentences from Wundt's *An Introduction to Psychology* (1912) expose a mature recognition of the meaning of More Is Different, a recognition of which Freud must have been aware.

Freud did seem, at times, to think in a More Is Different mode when facing issues that concern the matter of the mind, going as far as doubting the potential contribution of any science or philosophy to the understanding of the relation between the psychical and the

[10] Wundt (1912, p. 188).
[11] Ibid, pp. 193–4.

physical. For instance, in *A General Introduction to Psychoanalysis*, a series of twenty-eight lectures read in Vienna (1915–17),[12] he says:

> Neither speculative philosophy nor descriptive psychology nor that so-called experimental psychology which allies itself with the physiology of the sense organs … is in a position to teach you anything useful concerning the relation between the physical and the psychical or to put into your hand the key to the understanding of a possible disorder of the psychic functions. Within the field of medicine, psychiatry does, it is true, occupy itself with the description of the observed psychic disorders and with their grouping into clinical symptom-pictures; but in their better hours the psychiatrists themselves doubt whether their purely descriptive account deserves the name of a science. The symptoms which constitute these clinical pictures are known neither in their origin, in their mechanism, nor in their mutual relationship. There are either no discoverable corresponding changes of the anatomical organ of the soul, or else the changes are of such a nature as to yield no enlightenment.… Here is the gap which psychoanalysis aims to fill. It prepares to give psychiatry the omitted psychological foundation, it hopes to reveal the common basis from which, as a starting point, constant correlation of bodily and psychic disturbances becomes comprehensible. To this end, it must divorce itself from every anatomical, chemical or physiological supposition which is alien to it.[13]

But Freud found it difficult, as many of his readers over the years realized, to take the More Is Different path throughout. His ambiguity – which might be read as an inability to let go of scientism and truly exercise the intellectual autonomy of depth psychology from physiology – surfaces here and there in his texts, and cannot be dismissed by relying on an "early" versus "late" Freud dichotomy.[14]

12 Gay (1998, p. 382).

13 Freud (1920, p. 9).

14 Peter Gay (1998, p. 78) writes – in the context of Freud's 1895 *Project for Scientific Psychology* – that "the physiological and biological substrata of the mind never lost their importance for Freud, but for several decades they faded into the

For instance, in *Beyond the Pleasure Principle* (also published in 1920), he seems to express a completely different stance toward the relations between psychology and physiology, as he writes: "The deficiencies in our description would probably vanish if we were already in a position to replace the psychological terms by physiological or chemical ones."[15] The charged wording – "already in a position to replace" – explicitly labels psychological theories as transient intellectual endeavors that will no longer be needed when brain physiology and brain chemistry mature, an idea reflected in the discourse around the turn of the millennium. This sentence is much cited by proponents of modern psychoanalytic biologism, but – as any reader of Freud knows – the volume of his writings is immense and, to our delight (this author's included), a selective choice of excerpts may serve whatever the politics of academic discourse requires.

Critical analysis of More Is Different in physics, and its reflection in discussions on the relations between brain and behavior, raises an issue that deserves consideration. Small (microscopic) and large (macroscopic) scales are physical measures applied to space and time, but here they are equated with categories of functional organization. Doing so is the consequence of blindly following the lead of both sides of the debate between particle and condensed matter physicists: the former believed that their fundamental laws would serve to explain such phenomena as biology[16] – the phenomenon of life itself – whereas the latter openly argued that what they have learned from the scale jumps between particle and condensed matter physics applies to scale jumps between levels as far apart as psychology and social sciences.[17] Leaving aside problems entailed by lack of metrics for estimating and comparing distances between such levels

background as he explored the domains of the unconscious and its manifestations in thought and act."

15 Freud (1920a, p. 60).

16 Weisskopf (1965).

17 Anderson (1972).

of organizations (how could one begin to contemplate comparing the distance between, for example, chemistry and biology to the distance between biology to psychology?), a more important question might justifiably be asked: in what sense are the dynamics of an organism's behavior *macroscopic* to dynamics of neural populations? Why do we naturally accept schemes, pervasive in neuroscience textbooks that show levels of organization hierarchies with behavior at the top floor and genes or cellular processes at the bottom, with intermediate levels occupied by brain, network, neuron, and synapse? If we search for an answer in the physical composition of things, such behavior-to-cell hierarchies cannot be justified throughout. Indeed, neurons are biological cells, built of genetic material and processes that realize their potential in the form of molecular dynamics within and across membrane-bounded spaces; disassembling a neuron to its components, one ends up with genetic material and many other kinds of atoms and molecules arranged in heterogeneous clusters, microscopic to the cell level. It is also obvious that neural networks are built of neurons that synaptically interact with each other; single neurons are the natural physical scale of the components from which a neural network is built. Brains are built of neural networks that interact with each other and are connected to sensors and muscles. But behavior is not built of brain. Breaking behavior down to its components does not naturally leave us with a brain at hand; this is probably the most formidable barrier for the dialogue, that is – the idea of extending forms of discourse that fit nearby levels to the jump between brain and behavior.

Hierarchical diagrams with behavior on the top floor and then brain, networks, neurons, synapses, and subcellular processes nicely layered one beneath the other, should be read as hierarchies of functional organizations. Single neuron activity may be thought of as a lumped functional organization of subcellular processes that interact within and across membrane-bounded spaces. A neural network's activity may be envisioned as a lumped functional organization of coupled neuronal activities, and the activity of the brain may be thought of as a lumped functional organization of interacting neural networks. Behavior may be thought of as a lumped functional organization of brain dynamics coupled to sensors and muscles that interact with the world. The scale of organization and the physical scale are not synonymous. Sometimes a scale jump in one corresponds to a scale jump in the other (for example, neuron to network), but this is not always the case (for example, brain to behavior, chemistry to biology, biology to life, and so forth). In the present text, Anderson's More Is Different is to be understood as related to scale jumps in the wider, organizational sense, beyond physical scales, even though his arguments are strictly based on the more limited and formally approachable case of the many-body physics. The term "scale" as used here refers to the wider sense that accommodates both meanings, restricting "physical scale" to the narrow sense.

Less Is Not Simpler

The funnel view relies on a conviction that, while at the macroscopic scale things seem mysterious, as we go down the scales to observe smaller and smaller spatial or temporal elements of the phenomenon, we expect matters to become clearer; the macroscopic phenomenological complexity reflects, according to this conviction, an aggregation of simpler-to-define spatial or temporal objects. It is plain why such a Less Is Simpler image seems natural: allegedly, human movements that produce language, art, technology, and so forth are more complex than the behavior of a neuron. Likewise, cellular organization is surely more complex than single protein molecules or atomic nuclei. But, what exactly is being compared here? What does one mean by "more complex"? Is the ability of a child to make a motor choice involving articulation more complex than the phenomenon of turbulence? Or the dual existence of an elementary physical entity as both a particle and a wave? How can such comparisons be made?

Closer to the subject matter of this essay, is there a dimension within which the complexity of human behavior, neural networks, single neurons, and single protein molecules can be compared?

The evasiveness of the concept of complexity is all too familiar; none of the many formal definitions of this concept is able fully to convey its nature. Yet, regardless of which metrics one chooses to apply in order to estimate how complex a given brain-behavioral phenomenon is, it turns out that the naive Less Is Simpler picture does not hold. Complexity goes all the way down the scales of functional organization, from behavior to brain, single neurons and single protein activity; the spatial and temporal complexity at these levels of organization is – for all practical matters – unbounded.[18] Complexity is reflected in scale-rich multiple and entwined variables, inability to account for observed phenomena by breaking them into pieces, as well as heterarchical relations between processes. As a consequence, connections between causes and effects cannot be collapsed to proportional, simple rules; this is often referred to as "non-linearity": minor stimuli may give rise to large effects over many time scales, large stimuli to small effects or no effects at all, and shifts among these "input–output" regimes are often reminiscent of swift phase transitions. Related to this, statistics – even the most basic (for example, average, variance) – refuse to assume definitive values; rather, they change as a function of the temporal and spatial resolution applied by the observer. Imagine that one is asked to measure and report *the* average time that a given process stays at state *X* before it moves to another state *Y*. For instance, the average time that the subject – or the brain of that subject, or a network within the brain, or a single neuron within the network, or a single protein within the

[18] Accessible texts related to the following discussion on the origins and consequences of complexity that goes all the way down include, for instance, Bassingthwaighte, Liebovitch and West (1994); Havel (1996); Noble (2006, 2008); Heylighen (2001); Marom (2010); Braun and Marom (2014); and references therein.

neuron – spends in a well-defined mode of activity before a switch to another well-defined mode occurs. At all these levels, and for the vast majority of activities of interest, the simple question – *What is the average time to switch from mode X to mode Y?* – does not have an answer. The time to switch between *X* and *Y* changes as a function of the temporal resolution one uses in measuring it – a phenomenon that is probably familiar to readers exposed to self-similarity in popular fractal objects (a mathematically related concept).

Other manifestations of complexity that go all the way down the ladder of functional organization, include the spontaneous emergence of macroscopic coherent behavior from local microscopic interactions (a phenomenon called "self-organization"), multiple feedbacks and distributed control, hierarchical cascades of bifurcations, adaptations in combinatorial large spaces, and the seemingly bizarre *downward causation*:[19] macroscopic levels of organization (for instance, a subject's behavior or a physiological phenomenon) dictating the dynamics of their lower microscopic components (for instance, neural activity or genome expression, correspondingly). None of these is compatible with the funnel view. Less is not synonymous with simple.

Reverse Engineering

More Is Different and Less Is Not Simpler entail several epistemological consequences. One such consequence concerns beliefs that are propagated in circles of neuroscientists and psychologists-turned-neuroscientists, beliefs that rely on the extraneous funnel view. The general argument goes like this: (1) neuroscience and psychology share the same objectives; (2) neuroscience is fundamental whereas psychology is phenomenological, therefore

[19] Among the other names used to express similar effects are: final causation, reversed causation, top-down causation, and right-to-left causation.

psychology should eventually be collapsed to (taken over, or explained away) by neuroscience; (3) reductionism, by means of reverse engineering, is the way to achieve this goal. A brief comment on this argument is made in light of our preceding discussions, focusing on the first and third statements; the falsity of the second statement (fundamental physiology and phenomenological psychology) comes out naturally from More Is Different.

The avowed motivation of brain sciences as verbalized in textbooks and monographs of writers in the field is wide. The following statement integrates what one finds in the opening sentences of such texts: *The goal of brain science is to understand the mental faculties, the various conscious and unconscious aspects of behavior – sensory and motor, emotional, and cognitive – in health and disease.* Read "understand the mental faculties" as being able to phrase a coherent argument, a cascade of physiological expressions that is consistent with the observed.

There are obvious overlaps between the objective of brain sciences, and that of psychology. Brain science and psychology are different disciplines (different languages, different means of investigation, different educational systems) that seem to have similar purposes. It is not obvious that identical objectives of two allegedly different disciplines is a unique situation in science; it is certainly not a bad thing, especially if one acknowledges scientific disciplines as languages about natural phenomena rather than the phenomena themselves (see Chapter 3). Many brain scientists believe that brain sciences and psychology, given these overlapping objectives, are to become one integrated discipline. The idea of an integrative discipline might work if the format of present day physics as an integrative science is adhered to: rooming levels of organization ranging from the most microscopic elementary processes to the most macroscopic, while respecting the intellectual autonomy of the different levels, in the Andersonian sense. Such integration is very demanding; while psychology and neurophysiology might overlap in terms of their stated objectives, they differ significantly in the ranges of scales to which their abstract or actual concepts and objects are applied – their scale horizons.[20] This state of affairs calls for a significant, maybe utopian, change in the culture of both physiological and psychoanalytical education, a possible but not guaranteed outcome of a mature dialogue that, to start with, acknowledges the very existence of scale horizons. However, reading through brain science literature published from around the year 2000 and onwards makes it very clear that the integrative brain-behavior science that is imagined by most active writers is different from this physics-like picture. What several influential circles of neuroscientists call "integration" is no less than collapsing the psychological to the biological by means of reverse engineering, the present time main road to reduction in biology.

Unlike the overloaded concept of reductionism, reverse engineering is a relatively well-defined procedure that exposes itself to critical analysis. It is common to think of reverse engineering in surreptitious contexts (military or industrial), yet the concept has a broader meaning in the language of technology, denoting the process of detailed examination of a functional system when facing a limited a priori knowledge of its design principles. In this sense we all do reverse engineering, trying to figure out the mechanisms underlying the observed.[21] But More Is Different and Less Is Not Simpler lead to serious difficulties in pointing at a relevant level of organization within which a mechanism is to be sought: to some, behavior may and should be mapped to the single neuron, single synapse, or even a single protein or a gene; to others it is large populations of neurons or global concentrations of chemicals. The multitude of possible mappings exposes the inherent difficulty of reverse engineering – its indeterminacy – a strong constraint on the entire endeavor of neuroscience; a constraint that we all,

[20] Scale horizon is a term coined by Ivan M. Havel in his insightful geometric metaphor (Havel, 1996); a qualitatively defined metric of scale richness, extending from "scale thin" systems that are characterized by one or few dense scales, to "scale rich" systems characterized by an unbounded continuum of observable scales.

[21] See Dennett (1995) for an interesting, related discussion.

too often, tend to ignore. From More Is Different we learn that it is not trivial, maybe even impossible, to infer the macroscopic order of an evolving complex system that interacts with the environment from its known microscopic structure and activity. Taken together with Less Is Not Simpler – the fact that spatial *and* temporal complexity are not reduced by going downwards to smaller scales – the idea of reverse engineering (and naive reductionism in general) is practically hopeless. Congruent with this logic, it has been repeatedly demonstrated that the application of reverse engineering to the study of functional biological "toy" systems with known (but concealed) design principles may result in a perfectly valid induction that is wrong from the point of view of the underlying principles.[22] These demonstrations of the indeterminacy of reverse engineering are not aimed at rediscovering the limits of inductive reasoning; rather, they offer us physiologists an exercise in modesty.

Experienced biologists committed to reverse engineering sometimes respond to these thoughts by saying: "Do you have an alternative? Otherwise, your claims are destructive!" to which one might reply that it is not in our (scientists') mandate to find reasons to do wrong things when the right things to do are unclear. Reverse engineering is a practical rather than Jamesian pragmatic process; if it succeeds in extracting a predictor that works, irrespective of its relation to the actual design principle, the process is considered successful and applicable. Unlike reverse engineering, the business of physiology and psychology *as basic sciences* is to uncover the actual design principles; this is where the naive implementation of reverse engineering fails.

Maybe the thing considered a major hindrance to reduction by reverse engineering is an integral, defining feature of living systems. In other words, the degeneracy that is inherent to biological systems by

[22] A point already made by Hopfield and Tank (1986) in their seminal paper on computing with neural circuits, and demonstrated by (for example) Lazebnik (2004); Krishnan, Giuliani and Tomita (2007); Marom et al. (2009); Kumar et al. (2013); Vlachos et al. (2013).

virtue of More Is Different and Less Is Not Simpler (in both space and time) is the very thing that enables development through evolution to cope with a multiplicity of functions and unforeseen challenges. As such, our limitation in reducing living systems by adherence to reverse engineering reflects our misconception of what a design principle in biology and the social sciences actually is.

I end this short section on reverse engineering in brain and behavioral sciences by commenting on a potentially related aspect that might have significant consequences. To many, the endgame of reducing brain-behavioral phenomena by means of reverse engineering is to integrate the resulting knowledge in a machine that thinks and behaves, maybe even becoming emotional, like a human. This was the original project of artificial intelligence: incorporation of brain research facts into computer programs might teach us something about the boundaries of the human mind. But in a world where More Is Different and Less Is Not Simpler, it is not at all clear what are the relevant brain research facts to be incorporated into the machine. One potential consequence of this is beautifully expressed by Garry Kasparov, the great chess master, in a short article published in *The New York Review of Books*.[23] Kasparov tells the history of his 1985 simultaneous play against thirty-two chess computers, achieving a perfect 32–0 score, winning every game. Eleven years later Deep Blue defeated him, and once again the year after. But Deep Blue did not win by playing like a human; it won by systematically evaluating 200 million potential moves every second, a brute-force number-crunching, which "was only intelligent the way your programmable alarm clock is intelligent," says Kasparov, a fact that is well-acknowledged by artificial intelligence specialists. With the proliferation of desktop computers and powerful chess software, the game became more popular than ever, a positive unintended consequence. The negative

[23] Garry Kasparov, "The Chess Master and the Computer," *The New York Review of Books*, Volume 57(2), published on February 11, 2010.

consequence is that the style of the game has changed. Playing against machines, says Kasparov:

> … has contributed to the development of players who are almost as free of dogma as the machines with which they train. Increasingly, a move isn't good or bad because it looks that way or because it hasn't been done that way before. It's simply good if it works and bad if it doesn't. Although we still require a strong measure of intuition and logic to play well, humans today are starting to play more like computers.

This is chess, a two-thousand-year-old game; but what is really challenged here goes far beyond – it is about human values, style, aesthetics, and romanticism, and the impacts of a dialectical process that steers the evolution of society and culture. The science-fiction concept of "technological singularity" comes to mind: the point in time where the intelligence of machines will become greater than human intelligence. Beyond the technological singularity, say those futurists and science-fiction people, human history is going to change in unimaginable ways. But – to the extent that Kasparov's observation holds – arrival at the technological singularity might be shortened by reducing human intelligence to machine-like intelligence, rather than humanizing the cogitative capacities of machines. "Like so much else in our technology-rich and innovation-poor modern world," says Kasparov, "chess computing has fallen prey to incrementalism and the demands of the market. Brute-force programs play the best chess, so why bother with anything else? Why waste time and money experimenting with new and innovative ideas when we already know what works? Such thinking should horrify anyone worthy of the name of scientist, but it seems, tragically, to be the norm." Indeed, such thinking threatens to dominate science, from policy making in the allocation of research funds[24] to the interpretation of semantically empty biomedical observations.[25]

24 As exercised in, for example, the European Human Brain Project and similar corporate science initiatives.

25 As often happens when categories in the Diagnostic and Statistical Manual of Mental Disorders (DSM) – meant to ease classification – are taken as entities, the coordinates of which are searched in brain images or genetic mutations.

Why Reduce?

The two tenets of the funnel view do not hold. Where More Is Different and Less Is Not Simpler, a picture of reductionism emerges, which the ironic words of a remarkable poet describe as an:

Island where all becomes clear.
Solid ground beneath your feet.
The only roads are those that offer access.
Bushes bend beneath the weight of proofs.
The Tree of Valid Supposition grows here with branches disentangled since time immemorial.
The Tree of Understanding, dazzlingly straight and simple, sprouts by the spring called Now I Get It.
The thicker the woods, the vaster the vista: the Valley of Obviously.
If any doubts arise, the wind dispels them instantly.
Echoes stir unsummoned and eagerly explain all the secrets of the worlds.
On the right a cave where Meaning lies.
On the left the Lake of Deep Conviction.
Truth breaks from the bottom and bobs to the surface.
Unshakable Confidence towers over the valley.
Its peak offers an excellent view of the Essence of Things.
For all its charms, the island is uninhabited, and the faint footprints scattered on its beaches turn without exception to the sea.
As if all you can do here is leave and plunge, never to return, into the depths.
Into unfathomable life.[26]

It is reasonable to ask ourselves, given this state of affairs, why it is we insist on explaining macroscopic complexity by superposing simple elements and processes. Why does it feel more convenient compared to a picture according to which complexity is delegated to elements

[26] Poem 'Utopia,' from *Poems New and Collected 1957–1977* by Wislawa Szymborska. Translated by S. Baranczak and C. Cavanagh. Copyright (1998) by Harcourt, Inc. Reprinted by permission of Houghton Mifflin Harcourt Publishing Company. All rights reserved.

and processes all the way down the ladder of reduction? Reliance on (and search for) uniquely defined, small-scale simple elementary biological processes as explanations of large-scale behavioral complexity, is a dominant method in modern science. For most of us, the very idea of a process that cannot be reduced to a set of states and well-defined state transitions is difficult to digest. Maybe, as Bridgman wrote in 1927, it reflects an "apparent demand of our thinking apparatus to be furnished with discrete and identifiable things to think about ... The mind seems essentially incapable of dealing with continuity as a property of physical things."[27]

But reduction is more than a consequence of incapability built into our thinking apparatus; it has a meaning. Reductionist scientists, at least those of us who care about the limits of our trade, provide three reasons to hold on to our course.

The first is purely aesthetic. Going down the scales of organization, observing smaller and smaller things, provides immense satisfaction, which results from repeated exposure of natural universals. The same forms of relations between components or processes are rediscovered at every level of observation, nested in scalar organization hierarchies. The laws underlying the formation of social networks are formally equivalent to the dynamic laws that govern the formation of cliques of ants and neural groups and cell membrane protein groups, and so forth. This is not a case of a microscopic law that governs macroscopic phenomena; rather, *forms* of relations between variables are similar. Justifying reduction on this aesthetic basis raises the question of why the brain or its constituents should be the codomain to which behavior is reduced. If the aesthetic value of reduction emerges from identification of analogous forms of relations between

[27] Bridgman (1927, pp. 93–4). Physics, of course, has gone a long way in developing techniques to deal with continuity since Bridgman's critical analysis was published; it is now our "thinking apparatus" that seems to lag behind, incapable of intuiting these remarkable achievements.

variables, reducing psychology to the dynamics of cliques of ants or to the dynamics of populations of magnetic spins, might (and in fact does) carry an aesthetic value that is as – or even more – rewarding.

The second motivation to exercise reduction is related to the task of exorcism, which science has taken upon itself in the 300–400 years of its existence: proving that the concept of God is superfluous, at least when the aim is to explain natural phenomena. However close one looks, however high the resolution at which one observes the human body, no spirits are found; just complex dynamics over complex matter. Paradoxically, the journey of naive reductionism that obsessively seeks for "discrete structures further and further down in the scale of things, whole *raison d'être* is to be found entirely within ourselves,"[28] is heavily infected by spirituality and is itself religious. How else should one interpret the search for a gene of adventure-seeking behavior or the neural network of romantic love? Searching for little demons and gods within ourselves reflects longings for some homunculus within "who knows"; the possibility that there is no one in (or out) there, that we are alone, is unbearable.

The third reason for a reductionist program is, to me, the most important. It is the solid, rigorous reduction pointing to Havel's scale horizon of relevance that characterizes different levels of organization.[29] The scale horizon of relevance is the range of scales within which variables, processes, concepts, and laws identified in a given level of organization are relevant for the construction of formal understanding. Scale horizon of relevance defines a soft border beyond which More Is Different. Viewed negatively, it is a border that certifies the impossibility of collapsing the macroscopic to the microscopic. Admittedly, identifying the limits of one's own findings does not seem a motivation for a scientist in an era that celebrates and promotes omni-potential statements. As pointed out by Havel,

28 Bridgman (1927, p. 93).
29 Havel (1996).

it is rather embarrassing for us scientists that our concepts and laws retain their meaning only in their neighborhood of scale dimension. Henri Atlan offers an interesting, Winnicottian escape route; unlike the naive reductionist whose aim is to literally explain everything from the bottom, a mature reductionist will invest himself in the project of reduction *as if* it were possible to explain everything from the bottom, while – at the same time – knowing that explanatory gaps will always remain. In his *Intercritique of Science and Myth*[30] Atlan describes the unavoidable tension that is inherent to such sober reductionism:

> The desire that science provide a comprehensive explanation plays the role, when one succumbs to it, of a temptation, lurking within scientific praxis, that is more appropriate to mysticism. It can be eluded through skeptical critique and the restoration of the requisite distance between even the most firmly established scientific theory (especially the most "established") and reality – by accepting the pluralist character of this approach, taking into account the plurality of scientific disciplines as they are practiced, always from bottom to top, but with white space, the "token" physicalism of the functionalists, or a weak reductionism, that is, without the support (?) of a unifying explanatory metaphysics; where the white spaces of language are accepted as being those that also divide the disciplines, while the dynamic of the process itself endeavors incessantly to overcome them – using language in which new white spaces appear.

Meaning resides in these white spaces, in the gaps between levels.[31] To remove the white spaces between psychology and physiology is nothing less than to dissolve the meaning of psychology and physiology. But there is still a way to go before this statement is comprehensible, even if controversial.

[30] Atlan (1993, p. 76).
[31] See also Atlan (1989).

Consequences

We have pushed ourselves into a corner. On the one hand, More Is Different and Less Is Not Simpler imply that adhering to reduction, at least in its naive form as expressed in dreams of reverse engineering the brain, is logically doomed. On the other hand, reduction, beyond being psychologically inevitable, seems rational: it is justified aesthetically, morally and, above all, as a means for drawing boundaries to knowledge, thus balancing the arrogance of brutal positivism. A possible way out of the conflict entails exercising mature reductionism, the hallmark of which is being willing to play the game while acknowledging the consequences of the scale horizon, as will be discussed.

Behavior, physiology, and psychology extend over wide spatiotemporal scales. The dimensions involved in behavior range from fractions of seconds to lifetime, millimeters to meters and far beyond. Physiological elements and their dynamics involve molecules, synapses, cells, and groups of cells, operating at an immense range of temporal scales. Processes at the single molecule level may take place on the nanosecond to the many hours scale; processes at the tissue level (e.g., brain region) may take place on the millisecond to days, weeks, months, and years scale. Psychological entities and their dynamics, normative or pathologic, also span a wide range of interactive scales: from incidental short events (for instance, slips of the tongue) to extended temporal and spatial processes (for instance, attachment, grief). Whichever way we look at these ranges, the gap between the smallest and the largest in behavior, psychology, and physiology is immense, reaching five to ten, and more, orders of magnitude. Arguing for relevancy of observables across such ranges is comparable to stating that the flows within a cup of tea are determinants of, taking part in, or determined by the generation of galactic flows.[32] We

32 This is not to say that forms of relations between small scale elements cannot teach us a lot on forms of relations between large scale elements; such metaphors, as already mentioned, are indispensable.

must bear in mind the danger attached to such extrapolations when reading reports on alleged causal relations between, for instance, a mutation in a given gene and the tendency of its human carrier to become depressed.[33] Further serious complications reveal themselves by acknowledging that these different scales are not necessarily (and conveniently) arranged in a hierarchical manner where each level is driven by its neighbor on the floor below, and drives the one on the floor above. In fact, direct links exist between levels of organization that are far apart, and – importantly – such couplings can take the form of a two-way communication. Molecular activities and behavior are dynamically linked, bi-directionally, giving rise to a whole spectrum of inabilities to tell causes from effects under such circumstances.[34]

A naive reductionist would probably be further dispirited when the very concept of physical scale is deconstructed. Let us elaborate this point, which was briefly mentioned earlier. While vaguely defined, the physical scale concept has an operational flavor. The answer to the question *What is the physical scale of an observed object or process?* is expected to be a number that designates characteristic length or characteristic time in the space of a system's configurations.[35] Equipped with a physical scale, one may decide on measurement and modeling strategies; for instance, how frequently in time an object or a process need be sampled to obtain a faithful reconstruction of its trajectory,[36] or how detailed the representation

33 Let alone when human depression is represented or "modeled" by inducing a change in lever-pressing behavior in mice, a scale jump in yet another dimension.

34 For an accessible overview of these forms of two-way communication the reader is encouraged to consult Denis Noble's *The Music of Life: Biology Beyond Genes*, 2006, or one of its sequels; for example, Noble (2008).

35 For example, in the psychological realm one might ask: *what is the time scale of an analytic process?* The expected answer is a number – a time scale of, say, couple of years – that characterizes the process.

36 For example, what would be considered a reasonable interval to assess the progress of the analytic process?

of the object must be when incorporated into a large-scale model. The usefulness of the physical scale concept in general system analysis is beyond doubt; however, its application to analyses of living systems is not a straightforward matter. To start with, the very question *What is the physical scale of object (or process) X?* implicitly assumes the existence of uniquely defined scales (or a range of scales) that are intrinsic to objects. In other words, it is assumed that these physical scales are separable from each other in the boundaries, and that they are inherent to the observed system rather than reflecting the ways the observer chooses to measure them. But are these assumptions ubiquitously justified in the context of living systems? If not, we face serious trouble, because much of the experimental work done in biological sciences in general, and neuroscience in particular, is aimed at exposing presumably intrinsic and uniquely defined physical scales; they serve as guides in the search for microscopic mechanisms, and as a basis for most of the models in the field. Another related potential difficulty arises from the fact that these physical scales do not reveal themselves to the observer as tangible forms to be compared with some standard. In fact, the measurement of a physical scale is an inferential process that involves identification of an observable that (with any luck) reflects the degrees of freedom of the system. In the biological sciences, inasmuch as data collected so far tell us, observables are often very remote from the system's degrees of freedom, and are mostly dictated by technological constraints. What is the meaning of the physical scale concept under such conditions?

The inevitable abstractions made by an observer when estimating physical scales, abstractions that are essential when dealing with these difficulties, stow away the fact that in behavioral and brain sciences, physical scales are very often not intrinsic to the observed system; rather, in many cases they reflect boundary conditions that are imposed by the observer through the measuring procedure. This is true at practically every level of organization, from molecules to behavior.[37] To be sure, at each of these levels, physical scales might be bounded from below by rather straightforward underlying physical constraints; the identification of these constraints is dependent upon successful applications of the physical scale concept. But beyond these lower boundaries, more often than not physical scales of brain and behavioral phenomena are rich and dense; so much so that they should be considered, for all practical matters, continuous and unbounded.

Given these constraining facts, should we expect – from the outset – that events we choose to observe and describe in a given microscopic scale be semantically relevant to structures and dynamics at scales that are many orders of magnitude apart? Of course, we are all familiar with the captivating "butterfly effect" mnemonic for how sensitive are trajectories of chaotic complex systems to small perturbations in the initial conditions. But this would be a problematic path to take; relying on sensitivity of complex systems to initial conditions, explanations to practically everything inside and around us boil down to the origin of the universe, a syntactically sound yet semantically empty statement. In brain sciences, such valid but empty statements are fairly ubiquitous, usually in the context of measured correlations between features at one dimension and phenomena in some other dimension.[38] There is nothing wrong in seeking correlations between dimensions as part of the scientific process. But when such correlations are presented as explanations or mechanisms without following a careful procedure that takes More Is Different and Less Is Not Simpler into account, we run the risk of collecting semantically empty explanatory statements; errors that are comparable to claims of understanding how an automobile is working by pointing at the perfect correlation between key switching and engine activity.

[37] See, for instance, Marom (2010), and references therein.

[38] For instance, DNA alteration, activity of molecules, cells, or brain regions, correlated to mood, personality traits, imagery content, and so forth.

Hence, we are back to the question of how much may be gained, semantically, by linking different scales within a given discipline, let alone between different disciplines. The question is difficult, elusive; especially if one aims to keep distance from philosophical belief systems, the various "-isms." There are many examples where clear, meaningful links can be shown between small-scale events and large-scale consequences; psychoanalytically oriented psychologists surely accept this: small-scale incidents (for example, seemingly minor rejection at a critical point, local in time, local in space) do lead to large-scale changes in behavior. But examples from physiology, where small-scale perturbations (genetic, metabolic) lead to large-scale deviations in the physiological realm, might serve us better in developing the discussion. Consider, for instance, the uniquely defined point mutation that causes cystic fibrosis, a mutation that accounts for over 60% of cystic fibrosis cases worldwide. The mutation is in a gene, the product of which is a protein that mediates transport of chloride ions across biological membranes, a fundamental process in the secretion of sweat, digestive juices, and mucus; the symptoms and signs of the disease are well-understood, direct consequences of the impaired chloride transport process. The story of understanding cystic fibrosis, from the clinical symptoms and signs, through system and cell physiology to genetic mutation, is undoubtedly an achievement; careful examination of the origins of this understanding may teach us something about mature reductionism. For clarity, let us briefly explain the pulmonary (lungs-related) side of the story. It begins with the understanding of the pulmonary system, its anatomy and physiology: how air flows in and out, why we need air, and how gas is exchanged between blood vessels and air-filled compartments in our lungs. It continues with the acknowledgment that airways must constantly be cleaned and debris must be cleared, else they become clogged, compromise breathing mechanics, and cater to accumulation of disease-causing organisms. Later on, physiologists uncovered how this clearance happens: the fact that airways, like practically all other hollow structures in our body, are covered from within by a special class of cells (epithelia). These cells secrete fluids at just the right viscosity, fluids within which debris is trapped. The fluids are continuously pushed up and out the body by well-understood ciliary movement. The process of secretion is also understood; its relation to diffusion of ions (chloride, sodium, potassium, and others) and consequent movement of water molecules (osmosis) probably constitutes the most formally understood biophysical machinery.

Much more can be said about the physiology of the pulmonary system, but the point is that there is a satisfactory description of the system in the relevant language – physiology – validated by congruence on many scales. Having this wonderful physiology at hand (that is, the relations between processes, the context) it is easy to see where things can go wrong. In fact, they can and do go wrong at many points. Cystic fibrosis is just one such case, where defects in the process of fluid secretion through epithelial cells compromise the function of the breathing system. Moreover, since epithelia-mediated secretion of fluids is something that occurs in several other bodily organs and systems, links between the different symptoms of cystic fibrosis were immediately established: they are all consequences of an impaired secretion process. And, finally, when a gene was identified that was mutated in many of the patients, and the gene product was identified (chloride membrane transport protein) – the quest for understanding cystic fibrosis in the majority of patients ended.

Note that the cascade of expressions related to cystic fibrosis within the relevant discipline – physiology – was fully uncovered before links to the microscopic genetic domain were attempted. Pulmonary physiology was known; we had a full, formal, scientific description of the system in the scale of physiology. Likewise, the facts of hereditary factors that lead to dysfunction of secretion, which in turn causes obstructions in several systems – all this was well understood. This physiological picture *is* the explanation of cystic fibrosis, imposing macroscopic constraints on the semantics of the microscopic, syntactic "local" case. The finding of a genetic mutation that leads to the formation of a defective chloride transport protein, crucial for secretion across biological membranes, is a local case that is validated by congruence with pulmonary physiology. Had we not had the physiology in hand, the fact of cystic fibrosis mutation would be syntactically true but semantically empty.

More generally, being able to affect system level structures or processes by intervening with a given microscopic structure or process says nothing about the nature of the system. Scientific explanations are not correlations between structures or processes, nor control over structures or processes. For instance, let us pretend that we know nothing about the pulmonary system or breathing, and that the only thing we do know is that there is a hereditary disease that causes lung infections and strange, salty tasting sweat. Let us also pretend that some technique has enabled us to identify a single genetic mutation that fully corresponds to the occurrence of the disease. Moreover, imagine that there exists a technical maneuver that enables correcting the mutation immediately after birth, thus curing the disease. Note that in this imaginary scenario we have both a correlation between a microscopic feature (mutation) and a macroscopic phenomenon (disease), as well as full control (cure by correcting the mutation). Do we understand the disease? Obviously no; to understand the disease is to understand its physiology. We do, at least, know what causes the disease, right? Syntactically – yes, it is the mutation. But semantically – no, we do not know; without knowing the physiological context we cannot understand why such a mutation, or other possible mutations for that matter, would lead to the disease. In some senses, to understand a system is to be able to contemplate all the different ways that might take it astray, based on the physiological picture underlying it. To claim understanding only because we have identified correlations with genes or chemical agents is equivalent to the metaphor where one claims understanding an automobile engine because one has identified a correlation (and control relations) between key switching and engine activity.

This discussion is not foreign to psychoanalysts. The ability to relax the anxiety of a patient by ongoing use of benzodiazepines, chemical compounds that interact with ionic fluxes across membranes of brain cells, is extremely useful. But it is semantically empty, amounting to practically no impact on our understanding of the processes underlying anxiety in general, and the anxiety of a given subject in particular. A similar argument is valid for the cases of pharmacological impacts of drugs used to relax psychoses, depression or – for that matter – fever.

Some might feel satisfied with identified correlations and established control; these are the scientists who are interested in applied research, technology, and its important applications for the sake of helping people carrying diseases. But basic scientists seek theoretical contexts. The full story of cystic fibrosis provides an example of such a context, where the exact, actual mutation is only a special case, hardly relevant from the scientific point of view, but highly relevant for the development of medically applicable technologies. Present day attempts to identify paths, from small-scale genetic and physiological structures to complex large-scale behavioral phenomena, lack such a context. This is where the logic of glossy reports on genetic mutations as causes of schizophrenia, depression, adventurous personality, sexual preferences, partner bonding, and styles of parenting or political affiliation, fails. Likewise, the search for a neural network of (for example) romantic love is meaningless. What is needed is a psychological theory of schizophrenia, depression, or any other behavioral phenomenon of interest, a theory that might provide constraints to physiology.

As already stated, this essay is about the potential impacts of psychoanalysis on neurophysiology; more specifically, it is about psychoanalytic constraints that might guide neurophysiologists in phrasing meaningful questions. While recent prolific trends that focus on exactly the opposite direction – physiological constrains to psychoanalysis – are beyond our scope, let us end this chapter with a short description of the debate that concerns this trend; it is teaching.

The conviction that brain measures are relevant to depth psychology is widely accepted, leading one of the most distinguished neurophysiologists ever, the Nobel laureate Eric Kandel, to call for reexamination and restructuring of the intellectual and institutional frameworks of psychoanalysis, providing it with a more scientific foundation through biology.[39] There is no harm in providing analysts with relevant scientific knowledge; after all, the founders of the discipline were trained physiologists and physicians, and were undoubtedly influenced by their backgrounds. If nothing else, such knowledge might enable analysts to employ informed critical evaluation of naive attempts to explain psychoanalytic concepts by pointing to brain areas or processes. There is also no harm in offering mappings between abstract physiological concepts and abstract psychoanalytic concepts. Whether or not such mappings can lead to significant impacts on the foundations of psychoanalytic theory is an open question. However, much (but not all) of the activity that followed Eric Kandel's call took a rather *concrete* path, correlating clinical observables or expressions of affect or social interactions to brain loci or processes. In recent years this activity – aimed (mostly) at analytic audiences – goes under the name of neuropsychoanalysis.[40] Constructing an integrated picture from the diverse literature that concerns this passionate initiative is impossible within the present

[39] For example, Kandel (1998, 1999).

[40] Kaplan-Solms and Solms (2000); Solms and Turnbull (2011); Laufer (2012); and references therein. While the name – neuropyschoanalysis – is new, attempts to correlate between personality or emotional or social interaction features and brain structures in humans and animals is, of course, not new. See, for instance, Damasio et al. (1994) where the story of Phineas Gage's brain damage and its analysis, published in 1868, is described. More recent attempts to map emotional features of behavior to brain structure and dynamics are reviewed in the writings of, for instance, LeDoux (1996, 2000) and Panksepp (1998, 2012).

text; this might be pardonable given the overwhelming breadth claimed by neuropsychoanalysis, covering "... *all* work that lies along the psychoanalytic/neuroscience boundary."[41] But neuropsychoanalysts' statements about the relevance of recent brain research observables to the field of psychoanalysis, both its intellectual and applied aspects, are debated within the analytic community.[42] In a particularly sharp paper, Blass and Carmeli (2007) summarize key arguments against the relevance of brain research to psychoanalysis *in principle*. They actualize their conceptual stance toward "neurologizing" trends in psychoanalytic journals by deconstructing dimensions of modern brain studies claimed to directly impact on the conceptual framework of psychoanalysis (memory, affect, dream, and theory of mind). They demonstrate that brain research findings along these dimensions cannot possibly contain *psychologically* meaningful aspects that constitute the subject matter of psychoanalysis. Blass and Carmeli go as far as stating that biologism might have negative impacts on the future of psychoanalysis. This criticism is serious, challenging, and cannot be easily dismissed.

I sympathize with Blass and Carmeli's perspectives regarding the impacts of naive biological approaches to depth psychology. As they comment in the opening to their article, the message is conceptual, independent of any particular neuroscientific finding. Blass and Carmeli boil down their arguments for why "psychoanalysis should be less interested than other fields are in physical correlates of experience" to two reasons, which may be read as: (1) uniqueness of the subject matter of psychoanalysis, and (2) its being beyond the scale horizon of physical or biological substance. With the latter point

41 Solms and Turnbull (2011).

42 For example, Karlsson (2010[2004]); Blass and Carmeli (2007); Carmeli and Blass (2013); Talvitie and Ihanus (2011). For an earlier clear and lucid call to resist attempts to tie psychoanalytic theory to a neurophysiological foundation, see Edelson (1984, pp. 111–120).

I have no problem; this is the essence of More Is Different and there are solid scientific grounds to it, as discussed in the present chapter. But I am concerned by the first point that – whether the authors intended it or not – might be interpreted as justifying the distancing of psychoanalysis based on misplaced uniqueness of the former. Blass and Carmeli write:

> The subject of psychoanalysis is not a clearly defined phenomenon. Its subject, the meanings of thoughts and experiences, are never fully contained by the specific thoughts and experiences which convey them, but rather are determined by an indefinitely broader human context in which these occur. The same thoughts, words, or ideas, will have different meanings depending on what preceded them, or what occurred as they were expressed. No field has made this point more apparent than psychoanalysis.[43]

What they seem to say is that – to use science jargon – psychological states are not local in time or in space; there are an unfathomable number of interacting variables at different levels, correlated over wide temporal scales, that determine the meaning of a psychological state. This is of course not unique to psychoanalysis. Nature is densely populated with such phenomena, characterizing complex networks of coupled elements from the most microscopic to the most macroscopic, physical, biological, and sociological. In accordance, there are many abstract mathematical and physical concepts and formalisms to approach these. It would be wrong sweepingly to dismiss science's relevance to psychoanalysis based on such misplaced uniqueness. The philosophical and psychological foundations of the psychoanalytic movement are solid enough to prevail over naive biologism without throwing out the baby (science) with the bath water (scientism). Thus, I concur with Blass and Carmeli, doubting whether the realization of Kandel's call *in its concrete form* as expressed in most

[43] Blass and Carmeli (2007, p. 35).

neuropsychoanalytic research reports[44] can match the level of abstraction entailed in the task of identifying abiding impacts of modern science on psychology in general and psychoanalysis in particular. Having said this, I do believe that modern science should and will impact on the conceptual framework of psychoanalysis, as the science of 150 years ago impacted on Freud and his associates when they conceived the discipline. But I suspect that this potential impact of modern science on the conceptual framework of psychoanalysis will not be the result of the kind of science exercised by most neuropsychoanalysts today, where subjective and intersubjective concrete mental experiences are correlated with concrete brain processes and loci. Rather, abstract and universal notions of modern mathematics, physics, chemistry, biology, cybernetics, and engineering – for instance, dynamical systems and their coupling, self-organization and critical phenomena, chaos, theories of control and system identification, distributed representations, and the development of complex hierarchical network dynamics – are (to my mind) far more relevant than rules of synaptic plasticity or activity of neurons in this or that brain area; at least when the theoretical foundations of psychoanalysis (as opposed to clinical work) are considered. Examples of such abstract approaches, exercised by leading psychoanalysts and neuroscientists, are to be found in the literature;[45] whether these should or not be tagged neuropsychoanalytic is less important. One might hope that neuropsychoanalysis, which is an admittedly an

[44] Solms and Turnbull (2011) position paper, entitled "What Is Neuropsychoanalysis?" is taken as a clear and authoritative definition of its objectives.

[45] For example, see Stolorow (1997) and Friston (2009) [as applied in Carhart-Harris and Friston (2010)] for two very different styles of attempted mappings between scientific concepts of such general type to the conceptual framework of psychoanalysis. The first (Stolorow's) is an example for physics concepts that are independent of brain research; the second (Cahart-Harris and Friston's) is an attempt to map concepts from physics to psychoanalytic theory, aided by brain activity measurements.

"infant" initiative in its modern incarnation, refines its objectives and style, maintaining mature and sober empiricism while keeping a distance from naive reductionism and overly concrete or omni-potent statements; opinion leaders in neuropsychoanalysis – taking the broad-church approach – state that there is space for such developments, at least to some extent.[46] From the point of view of the present essay, in which the arrow of impact being sought is the inverse of the one that concerns most neuropsychoanalysts, the debate surrounding the trends of incorporating neuroscience into psychoanalysis is teaching; it points to the challenge of proper abstraction as a prerequisite for mappings of concepts between disciplines.

Recapitulation

One sentence phrased by a perceptive intellectual conveys the idea that I have tried to deliver in so many words: "For every problem there is an adequate scale, you do not want to read the newspaper with a microscope," said Valentino Braitenberg (1926–2011),[47] an admired neuroanatomist. To understand the meaning of a word, the relations between letters or phonemes must be considered; the meaning of a word is very sensitive to perturbations at these levels. But understanding a sentence calls for analysis of predication relations between different words; the meaning of a sentence is highly sensitive to perturbations of these predications, but much less sensitive to perturbed letters and phonemes. When a whole paragraph is considered, the adequate scale is that of relevancy relations between sentences; the meaning of a paragraph is less sensitive to perturbations at the level of predication within a given sentence, and even less so to perturbations at the level of letters. As we go up the scale of organization, meaning is constrained by relations with more (other) entities; the

46 For example, Solms and Turnbull (2011).
47 Moshe Abeles, personal communication.

scale horizon of relevancy changes, gradually recruiting new macroscopic observables, forgoing syntactically valid but semantically empty, irrelevant microscopic facts.

The myth of the funnel view, More Is Different, Less Is Not Simpler, the precarious path of reverse engineering, and their consequences imply that it is not immediately obvious how depth psychology and physiology should approach and constrain each other, if at all. The art of avoiding the epistemological crisis that is inherent to naive reductionism in current physiology–psychology rapprochement critically depends on the capacity of psychoanalysis to acknowledge realistically the strengths and – more important – the weaknesses of the logic of science, and to respect its own intellectual autonomy. Clearly, theories of depth psychology cannot be explained away by physiology. As for us physiologists, should we insist on reducing depth psychology to neural structures and activities, we would run the risk of being left alone on Szymborska's charming island, gazing as "faint footprints scattered on its beaches turn without exception to the sea … into the depths. Into unfathomable life."

An alternative, relational dialogue between psychoanalysis and neurophysiology is wanted, a dialogue that respects the white spaces, the gaps between levels. The next chapter (Chapter 3) presents both physiology and psychology as languages about behavior, languages between which a relational dialogue, pragmatic in the Jamesian sense, may be developed. The chapters that follow (Chapters 4–6) make use of the relational dialogue between languages in an attempt to import constraints from the psychoanalytic theory into the language of physiology, *for the sake of physiology.*

3 Language Relations

A dialogue between depth psychology and physiology is a dialogue between two discourses in languages that describe different, limited aspects of the same wider world of phenomena: the human body and its interactions with the environment, perceived through our senses or their artifactual extensions. As in all other languages, there are standards – some strict, others more relaxed – that define what is and what is not considered a valid statement within psychoanalysis and within physiology. For instance, a statement arguing that the unconscious is irrelevant to the understanding of overt human behavior is considered invalid within the psychoanalytic language. Similarly, a statement about muscular force that violates established principles of mechanics is considered an invalid physiological statement. The invalidity of a statement within a given language does not exclude the possible validity of that same statement in some other language. It is sensible to refer to (for example) "inner divine light that motivates our psychical life" in several languages, but definitely not within the language of psychoanalysis or within physiology. Thus, a dialogue between physiology and psychoanalysis is a dialogue between languages that are governed by standards. Not all the standards used are definable at present; but the ideal in the eyes of those who speak these languages is to base them on well-defined standards. In that sense, physiology and psychoanalysis are systematic, structured languages.

Systematic languages differ in the extent to which they lend themselves to formulation. At the one extreme are the formal languages, wherein things are well defined. More relaxed systematic languages are situated at the other extreme, housing objects that resist precise definition, objects that remain "sort of defined." While psychoanalysis is closer to the latter when compared to physiology, both – due to the nature of their subject matter – are very far from the extreme of formal systematic languages, such as mathematics and computer science. The following pages present a short overview on the structure of systematic languages in the context of physiology and psychoanalysis. Many possible paths offer a view of psychology and physiology as languages, most of which are philosophically based. However, the path taken is that offered by a distinguished mathematical biologist, Robert Rosen (1934–98), in his analysis of the life sciences.[1] Rosen's didactic introduction to model relations[2] is slightly adapted to the intended readership of the present essay; it begins with syntactic aspects, followed by the incorporation of meaning into a given language, and ends with the nature of relations between languages.

A word before diving in: Almost every scientific monograph has those pages where a combination of disappointment and annoyance is felt. Usually, these pages are embedded in the second or third chapter and have a technical (yet trivial) flavor to them; an anticlimax that follows a chapter or two that build up expectations. In writing the following pages, I felt that these are the ones that might cause annoyance, maybe leading readers to abandon the essay altogether. Nevertheless, the pages were left as they are, because it makes sense to expose the image one has in mind regarding scientific languages and their relations in general before contemplating a dialogue between them. The advice to the reader is this: "As the art of reading (after a certain stage in one's education) is the art of skipping …,"[3] readers

[1] Robert Rosen is the author of *Fundamentals of Measurement and Representation of Natural Systems* (1978), *Anticipatory Systems* (1985), *Life Itself* (1991), and other contributions to theoretical biology.

[2] Rosen (1991, ch. 2 and 3).

[3] James (1950[1890], Volume 2, p. 369).

who are familiar with these technical matters and intuit their applicability to physiology and psychoanalysis, or lose patience, should leaf through these pages and continue from the Section "On Abstractions in Physiology and Psychology," or skip this chapter altogether.

Syntax, Physiology, and Psychology

Physiology and psychoanalysis are systematic languages that are based on underlying assumptions and means to derive valid inferences. The *underlying assumptions* are "axiomatic" expressions, in the sense that they do not evolve from within the language. They are sets of beliefs that may (but need not) be supported by reference to things outside the language. For instance, the statement that human behavior is mostly a deterministic outcome of psychic history-dependent processes that interact with present sensory input is an underlying assumption of psychoanalysis. It is not proven or derived from within psychoanalysis. In fact, there cannot be a procedure to derive it from within psychoanalysis, because all known psychoanalytic statements are themselves derived – in one way or another – from this underlying assumption of behavioral determinism. The language of physiology also relies on axiomatic underlying assumptions, expressions that are not entailed by anything from within physiology. For instance, the statement that brain processes cannot contradict the laws of physics is an underlying assumption. One cannot derive this statement from within the language of physiology; this underlying assumption stems from a wider discourse that encompasses issues far beyond physiology.

We will not further elaborate on assumptions underlying neurophysiology and psychoanalysis, beyond saying that no genuine or useful dialogue between languages can take place if their underlying assumptions exclude each other. Intellectual alienation is an all too familiar experience for scholars attempting to map between languages that rely on incompatible underlying assumptions. The personal histories of the founders of psychoanalysis ensure that its underlying assumptions are compatible with those of natural sciences in general, and physiology in particular; Breuer, Freud, Jung, and many of their apostles were physicians and physiologists, imprinted by science at early stages of their education.

Inferences are derived from within the language as extensions of underlying assumptions and other inferences. Consider, for instance, the concept of "transference analysis," which is inferred from (and defined by) other expressions of the psychological language. We read Kernberg's definition, which serves as well as any other in the present context: "Transference analysis consists in the analysis of the reactivation in the here-and-now of past internalized object relations."[4] Transference analysis expressed as such is not an underlying assumption in the language of psychoanalysis; rather, it is the outcome of some manipulation of the concepts of internalization, object relations, reactivation, and (one might add) here-and-now as well as analysis. Without these other concepts within the language of psychoanalysis, the concept of transference analysis cannot be inferred. Likewise in the language of physiology: for example, homeostasis – a generic physiological concept that relates to controlling the internal environment, maintaining a stable metabolic equilibrium – is not an assumption; it is an inferred concept, entailed by the concepts of metabolism, equilibrium, control, and internal environment, among others.

The assignment of inferences to objects outside the language is discussed in the context of semantics, but already at this point it is acknowledged that the absence of a relation to the outside world does not in itself disprove the validity of an inference within a language. In fact, most inferences within a systematic language do not have referents in the world of sensed phenomena (taken to the extreme in the case of mathematics). The validity of an inference is dictated only by

[4] Kernberg (1987).

its consistent and congruent relations with the underlying assumptions and the other inferences within the language. Whether or not the concept of transference is related to something in the world of sensed phenomena is an important question; but the answer to that question does not impact upon the validity of the concept within the language of psychoanalysis. Likewise in physiology, the concept of homeostasis is valid whether or not there are tangible, sensed phenomena to which the concept is assignable.

Each given inference descends from preceding inferences or underlying assumptions, and may – in turn – give rise to new inferences. Of course, in psychology and physiology it is rare to find strong generative relations between inferences such as "if *A* then *B*"; the more often encountered relation between two expressions in these languages goes something like "given *A*, it is *likely* that *B* follows" (in a shorthand form: *A*→*B*). Often, this imprecise nature of inferences in psychology is held against its being treated as a scientific discipline. But psychologists might be surprised to learn that such maybe\might-be statements also densely populate the language of physiology, in spite of its scientific aura. Intensive clashes, within and between physiology and psychoanalysis, originate from the manner in which vagueness (i.e., maybe\might-be statements) is handled. For our purposes, it suffices to say that there are well-founded ways to live with probabilistic generative relations and remain "scientific," giving room for seemingly vague sentences such as "Anxiety is a *likely* outcome of Conflicts."

Whether being an underlying assumption or an inference, a small number of expressions in a fine systematic language have a unique stance, serving as *production rules*. A production rule is a mechanism, a means to derive an expression from other expression(s); a way to generate inferences. In terms of the arrow notation (*A*→*B*), a production rule is the thing that stands "behind" the arrow, the procedure allowing us to write down an arrow that leads from one statement to another. For instance, a production rule that is often (yet seamlessly) used in psychoanalysis is that of association by simultaneity.[5] This is the assertion that if two events are close to each other in time and (or) space, there is an increased probability that their impacts on the psychic life might be coupled; future occurrence of one might lead to a (subjective) experience of the other. In physiology, many production rules reflect relations between different forms of physical energy; but there are other, less well-defined production rules, such as the equivalent of the aforementioned psychoanalytic association by simultaneity. It states that when two neurons are active in spatiotemporal proximity, the probability that these neurons will form some sort of effective connection is expected to change. This production rule is heavily relied upon in neurophysiology and will be discussed in a later chapter dedicated to relational dynamics in physiology.

Where generative relations are concatenated (for example, *Conflict→Anxiety→Repression*), each of the cascade's elements may also be an element in other cascades; for example, anxiety might also be part of the generative relation cascade *Trauma→Anxiety→Rage*. This fact complicates matters immensely: inferences might converge, split, loop, terminate, or continuously evolve, constituting hierarchical or heterarchical topologies at various scales.[6] Contemplating a systematic language with underlying assumptions, inferences, and production rules, the image I have in mind is that of a complex network, with vertices representing inferences and edges representing generative relations. Others might prefer imagining the systematic language – in its present context – as a dynamical system with initial conditions (underlying assumptions), states (inferences), and dynamical (production) rules. Each representation, the complex network graph or the dynamical system, serves our purposes equally well.

5 Originally coined by Freud in the *Project for Scientific Psychology* (1950[1895], p. 319).

6 A heterarchy is a system of organization with intractable ascendancy, a form of organization resembling a network, where dominance is determined by context; in contrast, hierarchy is an organization where each level is subordinate to the one above it, regardless of context.

Working through physiology as well as psychoanalysis is an iterative sequence of applying production rules to underlying assumptions and inferences in order to generate new valid inferences. The utopia is that, at some point in the future, all possible valid expressions that may be made within a language are derived. Of course, science is now developed enough to acknowledge that such a complete coverage of all true expressions within a systematic language is inherently, mathematically impossible. Moreover, the Kuhnian concept of paradigm shift is suggestive of no less than a dramatic change in the very content of underlying assumptions, as part of a natural evolution of any scientific language.

Finally, the challenge of creating and developing a fine systematic language is in minimizing the number of underlying assumptions and production rules, while maximizing the number of inferences. It is not at all attractive to add an underlying assumption or to invent a production rule in order to overcome apparent inconsistencies or logical gaps. Indeed, the extent to which a language may be compressed in a lossless manner to essential axioms and production rules is a measure of its usefulness, validity, and aesthetics as a scientific endeavor. No physiologist or psychologist is naive enough to expect compression to a degree of mathematical *nirvana* – one assumed production rule applied to one axiom from which everything else is derived. Yet this utopian gold standard is out there, like a lighthouse: you do not wish to bump your ship into it, but it is an essential, welcomed guide when sailing in unknown waters.

Semantics, Physiology, and Psychology

The art of being wise is the art of knowing what to overlook.[7]

Being languages, psychoanalysis and physiology are not by themselves the phenomena of behavior they seek to describe; they are

[7] James (1950[1890], vol. 2, p. 369).

about these phenomena. Hence, the meaning of psychoanalysis or physiology amounts to the relations between statements within these languages and entities outside the languages, in the world of sensed phenomena. To analyze these relations, a definition of behavior in the wider sense, capturing both the physiology and the psychology points of view, is wanted. To this end we follow James's lead. In the prefatory chapter to *The Meaning of Truth*, James offers his empiricist stance: "The only things that shall be debatable among philosophers shall be things definable in terms drawn from experience. (Things of an unexperienceable nature may exist *ad libitum*, but they form no part of the material for philosophic debate.)"[8]

It is a somewhat humbling experience to acknowledge that when stripped of ostentatious aspirations, the only source that is available for us to say something about a person's behavior is the pattern of his/her movements, examined on different scales of time and space (fractions of seconds to lifetime, fractions of millimeters to thousands of kilometers). Movement here is meant in the wider sense: from simple grasping of an object, to a person's choices in life that are expressed as body movements in the world, or as words generated by movements of vocal chords. If a thing is not expressed as a pattern of movement in that wider sense, it is practically not a behavioral entity. This seemingly narrow definition of behavior (that is, whatever is expressed in patterns of present or future movements) encompasses things that might at first sight seem completely unrelated to movement. For instance, concepts such as resistance or conflict exist as behavioral entities only to the extent that they are expressed in words (vocal chords movements) or patterns of body movements, within the spatial and temporal scales of a therapy session or over days and more, outside the room.

We assume that behavior, defined as patterns of movements, follows perceivable regularities; that is, rules that are (in principle)

[8] James (1909, p. 826).

available to our understanding.[9] Such rules relate present behavior to some previous behavior and interactions with the environment. This does not exclude the possibility of random or irregular or unexplainable aspects in human movements; it simply implies that movements that are completely unrelated to any previous or future movements, while they might be interesting to document and characterize, cannot be the main subject matter for science.

To assume regularities in an individual's behavior is to assume generative relations between the movements of that individual, in the very same sense of inferential generative relations schematized in our discussion on the syntax of language. Thus the totality of a person's behavior may be viewed as a complex network that depicts all generative relations between this person's movements, those that actually occurred and those that might occur.

Of course, contemplating behavior in these simplistic terms unfolds an immensely complex network of possible generative relations between behavioral entities: every given movement is the result of previous movements of the observed person, as well as the collection of interactions with the environment (which is, in itself, a composite collection of movements of objects and subjects – the observer included – in the world). With such spatiotemporal immensity in the background, an attempt to plot a graph of generative relations between movements of a given person would be senseless. Instead, what is needed is a "good enough" description of the subject matter. It is difficult to resist re-citing what has become a cult reference in certain circles of neuroscientists; this is Borges's note on the Exactitude in Science:[10]

> In that Empire, the craft of Cartography attained such Perfection that the Map of a Single province covered the space of an entire City,

9 This is the Natural Law in Rosen's *Life Itself* (1991, pp. 58–9), without which, Rosen says, there is neither science nor scientists.

10 Borges, *A Universal History of Infamy* (1975).

> and the Map of the Empire itself an entire Province. In the course of Time, these Extensive maps were found somehow wanting, and so the College of Cartographers evolved a Map of the Empire that was of the same Scale as the Empire and that coincided with it point for point. Less attentive to the Study of Cartography, succeeding Generations came to judge a map of such Magnitude cumbersome, and, not without Irreverence, they abandoned it to the Rigours of sun and Rain. In the western Deserts, tattered Fragments of the Map are still to be found, Sheltering an occasional Beast or beggar; in the whole Nation, no other relic is left of the Discipline of Geography.

What Borges allegorically tells us extends far beyond a sharp criticism of naive reductionism. It is about scales and understanding, theory and modeling; it is about the meaning of science in the natural manifold of space and time. As Borges so vividly explains in a short text on *Ireneo Funes* (a man who detailed himself to death by filling his world with an evergrowing, immense set of contiguous particulars): "To think is to Ignore Differences, to Generalize, to Abstract."[11] Having said that, behavior may still be viewed as a graph, provided that we abandon dreams of complete and deterministic descriptions, and be satisfied with a good enough graph. What is good enough in our context? An answer to this question, partial as it may turn out to be, is something to which a deferential dialogue between physiology and psychology might contribute. Meanwhile, let us keep imagining behavior as a graph that depicts probable generative relations between groups of a given individual's movement patterns, as well as between relevant groups of movements of objects and subjects in the immediate environment of that individual. As will be shown, by holding to the graph metaphor, the possibility of partial mapping is unfolded, between generative relations of movements in the world of behavior, and generative relations of expressions in the languages of physiology and psychoanalysis.

[11] Borges, *Funes, His Memory* (1998).

Congruent Interpretation–Projection Cycles

When a claim is made that a given behavioral pattern is explained, be it by psychoanalytic or physiological language, what it actually means is that a given cascade of movements is mapped to a cascade of expressions in the language. Consider, for instance, a person within a psychotherapy session. Suppose that he suddenly complains that his heart rate has increased, his breathing is accelerated, and that he has "no air"; he then says that he forgot to mention that he must leave earlier today due to some prior commitment, gets up, and leaves (twenty minutes before the end of the session), answering an unasked question by stating that "everything is in order." All these phenomena – complaining, accelerated rate of heartbeat and rapid breathing, leaving the room, and so forth – are movement patterns, at different spatial and temporal scales. If a physiologist is asked to explain this cascade of movements, the response would probably sound as follows (just listen to the music, do not bother going into the details): *An increased secretion of adrenaline led to a cascade of fairly well understood cellular and systemic reactions, including amplification of pacemaking conductance in cardiac cell membranes (which translates to an accelerated rate of heartbeats), rapid breathing and probably sweating* [indeed, the therapist recalls that the patient started sweating before he got up to leave the room]. *The patient must have been pale and felt dizzy, since adrenaline causes constriction of blood vessels* [indeed, the therapist recalls now that his patient became pale and when he got up from his chair he leaned on the wall for a moment, as if about to pass out].

The physiologist, in his attempt to explain what happened to the patient, has mapped the cascade of movements (the domain of behavior) to expressions in the language of physiology. He started by interpreting the behavioral setting, translating it to an initial expression ("an increased secretion of adrenaline"), and from this point onward he applied valid physiological production rules to derive inferences (for instance, "adrenaline causes constriction of blood vessels"). The physiologist's interpretation is validated by an apparent congruence between the cascade of physiological inferences and the cascade of events in the behavioral domain (for example, "the patient must have been pale and felt dizzy").

While the same set of patient's movements (complaining, accelerated rate of heartbeat and rapid breathing, leaving the room, and so forth) may be read and explained in a completely different language by a psychologist, the process of partial mapping and validation by congruence is similar:[12] *This was an anxiety reaction, evoked by something that happened just before the patient started complaining. The patient provoked the therapist into what he perceived as an intimidating stance. The patient could not stand the entailed conflict; he was flooded by the impacts of his fearful but defiant internal relationship, in which one aspect of ego was locked in battle with another split-off aspect of ego identified with a bullying father representation.* Here the psychologist, like the physiologist, starts by interpreting the behavioral setting, translating it to an initial expression (anxiety), and applies valid psychological production rules (for example, looking backward along the timeline of the session: "evoked by something that happened just before") to generate inferences (intimidated; internal relationship, and so forth). The psychologist's interpretation is validated by the apparent congruence between the cascade of his inferences and the behavior of the patient in the past as well as here-and-now.

In both examples described, the explanation provided by the physiologist or psychologist is validated by the existence of congruence between the cascade of movements and the cascade of expressions in the language used. On the one hand we have behavior, that is, generative relations between movements; on the other there is the

[12] The following text is inspired by an example from Thomas H. Ogden, *The Matrix of the Mind* (1986, pp. 151–2), distorted for present didactic purposes.

language (be it psychology or physiology), that is, generative relations between linguistic expressions. The relations between these two systems may take quite complex dynamical forms, but we concentrate on the basics. The process starts with an observed movement in the behavioral system being mapped to an expression in the linguistic system. An important thing to note regarding this act of mapping is that it cannot be justified by anything within the two systems; not from within the language system, nor from the observed behavior. In other words, the question "Why is behavior *X* mapped to the language expression *A* and not to any other?" does not have an a priori answer. The choice of mapping behavior *X* to language expression *A* is an act of *interpretation*.[13] The physiologist interpreted the behavioral state of the patient as increased adrenaline secretion (an expression in physiology); he could have interpreted the state of the patient as *angina pectoris*, a clinical symptom indicative of coronary artery disease. The psychologist interpreted the same behavioral state of the patient as anxiety (an expression in psychology); he could have interpreted the state of the patient as *claustrophobia*. Any of these interpretations must (and can only) be validated by their pragmatic consequences. Within the language system, a cascade of expressions is derived, starting from *A* and may (theoretically) continue *ad infinitum*. The cascade is truncated at some point – expression *B*, for instance – the choice of which reflects a collection of beliefs (that will be addressed later on). Once truncated, the resulting linguistic expression *B* is mapped back onto a defined movement within the behavioral system, an act that may be denoted *projection*.[14] Projection, as interpretation, cannot be entailed by anything within the behavioral or the linguistic domains. But, if movement *Y* is entailed by movement *X* we can say that $A \rightarrow B$ is congruent to (or, a good enough

13 Rosen's encoding process, *Life Itself* (1991, p. 60).
14 Rosen's decoding process, ibid.

description of) the behavior $X \rightarrow Y$.[15] The cycle of interpretation (that is, mapping from behavior to the systematic language) and projection (that is, mapping back from the systematic language to the behavioral world) is the way by which meaning is attributed to language statements, a way to introduce semantics into a language. Validation by congruence is achieved through a process of formulation that must include a complete interpretation–projection cycle.

The concept of validation by congruence is "A New Name for Some Old Ways of Thinking" – as James subtitled his book *Pragmatism*.[16] There, and in his later text on *The Meaning of Truth*,[17] James urges the reader to embrace a stance according to which "Truth … is simply a collective name for verification-processes." Truth is not something that resides out there, attached to things and waiting to be discovered; truth is dependent on a process that takes place within the knower's mind:

> True ideas are those that we can assimilate, validate, corroborate and verify. False ideas are those that we cannot.… The truth of an idea is not a stagnant property inherent in it. Truth happens to an idea. It becomes true, is made true by events. Its verity is in fact an event, a process: the process namely of its verifying itself, its veri-Fication. Its validity is the process of its valid-Ation.[18]

Pragmatism expresses itself in modern ideas that span a wide spectrum of disciplines. These include the relations between formal systems and natural systems, and a whole world of modern frameworks

15 We assume that there can be many different ways to walk from one point to another within each of these behavioral and formal worlds. For instance, in the network of language expressions the order of arguments leading from one inference to another is not unique. Likewise in the case of the behavioral system; there are many different ways to go from one behavioral state to another. This multiplicity of possible realizations is ubiquitous and of paramount importance for any dialogue on brain and behavior.

16 James (1907).

17 James (1909).

18 Ibid.

that are meant to explain behavior in terms of "active sensing," "perception–action cycle," "predictive brain models," "top-down sensory processing," extensions of John Dewey's 1896 seminal paper on "The Reflex Arc Concept in Psychology" to which we will dedicate space in reviewing the origins of the functional stance in psychology. Moreover, understanding truth as a process of validation by congruence is an invaluable tool in the analysis of mechanisms underlying the formation and adaptation of psychological and physiological objects, as will be discussed in Chapters 4 and 5.

It is not too rare to find occasions in brain and behavioral sciences where interpretation is exercised without projection; this is the hallmark of mapping a behavioral entity to (for instance) brain coordinates or a set of well-defined genes. Likewise, cases of projection without interpretation are quite pervasive; consider, for instance, the field of psychopharmacology where the fact that modulating the activity of a given protein (generative relations in the physiological domain) entails a change in behavior (this is projection) is taken as evidence for the biological basis of the observed behavior. The fact that drugs that trim down the activity of dopamine receptor proteins in the brain also restrain psychotic symptoms was naively taken as evidence for an overactive dopaminergic system as a biological basis of psychoses; this is projection without interpretation. Maybe the dopamine hypothesis is now acknowledged as being naive, but just to the point of replacing over-active dopamine system with under-active glutamate system, the present psychopharmacological celebrity. By definition, such incomplete cycles cannot be validated by congruence; this is bad science. Of course, substandard practice of that sort is also found in psychoanalysis; maybe this is what Freud had in mind when he coined the term "wild" to designate an incomplete analytic procedure,[19] which – by definition – cannot be validated by congruence.

[19] Freud (1910, pp. 219–28).

On Abstraction in Physiology and Psychology

> *Truth is the same to us all; yet to each her appearance will vary.*
> *When she remaineth the same, diff'rent conceptions are true.*[20]

While contemplating the attribution of meaning by partial mapping of behavior to physiology or psychoanalysis, there is an aura of Jamesian "stubborn, irreducible facts" surrounding the former, as opposed to the latter. This aura is rooted in our (physiologists' as well as psychologists') academic education. It is taken for granted that physiological statements that result from measurements with instruments and expressed as mathematical equations are directly related to entities in the sensed world; certainly more than the apparently abstract, somewhat vague statements of psychoanalysis. So much so that prominent figures in the history of psychoanalysis fell into the imbroglio of seeking scientific approbation by expressing psychological inferences using Greek letters and mathematical relations. But psychologists might be surprised to learn that the apparent difference in the exactitude of these languages is an illusive faith that reflects a gap of spatiotemporal scales rather than scientific rigor. In subsequent chapters, we will learn that many (maybe most) perfectly valid physiological inferences require quite a stretching of the imagination, no less than the wildest of Freudian interpretations. This is because measurement itself, the tenet of solidity in the natural sciences, is the most significant act of abstraction in the making of science. This point is nicely expressed by Robert Rosen in his analysis of the life sciences, a body of theoretical work from which many of the concepts presented in this chapter are derived:[21]

> There can be no greater act of abstraction than the collapsing of a phenomenon down to a single number, the result of a single

[20] *Goethe and Schiller's Xenions* (1915[1797]).
[21] Rosen (1991, p. 60).

> measurement. From this standpoint, it is ironic indeed that a mere observer regards oneself as being in direct contact with reality and that it is 'theoretical science' alone that deals with abstractions.

Analogy to the "hard facts" of physiology and the "abstract" nature of psychoanalysis is not too demanding; both are predisposed to the inherent hazard of reification – the fallacy of misplaced concreteness, or the seemingly opposite, but actually the same, fallacy of "misplaced abstraction."[22]

As presented here, the dialogue between psychoanalysis and physiology is a dialogue between two languages that describe different, admittedly limited aspects of the same world of behavioral phenomena. In this sense, each of these languages is a model of behavior. An immediate consequence of an exposition of psychoanalysis and physiology as languages or models of behavior is that the dialogue is between two languages that have underlying assumptions, production rules, and inferences that might be very different from each other. These differences are reflected in the seemingly incompatible music that one hears when listening to an analyst speaking the language of psychology and to a physiologist speaking the language of physiology, even when they both describe the same set of movements.

That psychoanalysis and physiology describe aspects of the *same* wider world of phenomena – behavior as expressed in movements – calls for a form of what Rosen describes as tripartite relations.[23] That is, validation by congruence between the two languages, assisted by their common congruence with the behavioral system; a procedure to map – not to point at causal relations between, nor to explain away or reduce one language (or model) to the other. While a potentially powerful constraint in the processes of formulating theories, Rosen's tripartite relations should be exercised with care: the fact that psychoanalysis and physiology describe aspects of the same world of

22 Barzun (1983, p. 62).

23 Rosen (1991, pp. 62–64).

phenomena does not necessarily entail the existence of a way to map one unto the other; the reason being that, as explained, the incorporation of meaning into these two languages unavoidably involves partial mapping to the world of observables. In other words, the two languages may relate to different features that are only linked by their co-incidence within the mapped object.[24] Imagine two instruments that measure features of apples, one that is sensitive only to colors (green, red, yellow, and so forth) and the other that is sensitive only to spatial extensions (size, volume, diameter, and so forth). While examining the same object, the measures obtained by these instruments belong to orthogonal categories; some apples are red, some are not; some red objects are apples, many are not. And, of course, the redness of an apple does not explain or reduce its spatial dimensions and vice versa. We must keep this in mind when contemplating a dialogue between neurophysiology and psychoanalysis; we should be ready to accept the possibility that such a dialogue might end up with a conclusion that the two languages are (by and large) orthogonal to each other, an epistemic achievement in its own right. But let us not reverse the order of our argument; after all the purpose of the present essay is to analyze the possibility of defining a space wherein neurophysiology is informed by psychoanalysis.

Probably the most formidable barrier that stands in our way to realizing a tripartite scheme, and thus identifying a space for dialogue, is the Borgesian manifold of spatiotemporal scales involved in behavior, physiology, and psychology; their unfathomable complexity[25] as described in Chapter 2. Given the impacts of the spatiotemporal manifold of scales on the nature of a possible dialogue, we must ask ourselves: which domains, within each of these two languages,

[24] Consider, for instance, the two formulations exemplified for the case of anxiety attack within a therapy session; it is difficult to imagine a procedure to commute between these two.

[25] The concept of unfathomable complexity is presented in Elsasser's *Reflections on a Theory of Organisms* (1998).

may or should be dialogued? The term domain is used here to denote a subset of related concepts within a given language, populated by cascades of generative relations that share a substantially overlapping scale horizon. Ideally, formal machinery is wanted that in some magical way aids in identifying the relevant scales at which cascades of generative relations are sought, described, and validated by congruence. Such formal machinery is currently not at our disposal; in its absence, the stage is open to category errors.

Indeed, a ubiquitous error committed in brain sciences is that of attributing explanations of a phenomenon of interest to processes or objects that reside in irrelevant scales – whether too big or too small. But, is there any procedure available for physiologists to point to a relevant level of organization (gene, protein, synapse, cell, network, brain area), a level that lends itself to validation by congruence with depth psychology? The fact of the matter is that – as explained in the introductory notes on language relations – mappings between one system and another (psychology to physiology, in our case) are acts of interpretations and projections that cannot be justified by anything within the mapped systems. Interpretations and projections reflect other, larger scale languages that envelop both psychology and physiology; the reign of environmental, sociological, and historical forces, constrained by available technologies.

Are we doomed? Sentenced to life imprisonment in a land of rationalized, ad hoc excuses for our scientific choices? Probably so, at least where neurophysiology and depth psychology relations are concerned. But we insist on maintaining the Winnicottian nature of playful science, so we turn to seek for heuristics. One such heuristic, which is seamlessly exercised in our iterative attempts to validate by congruence, involves estimating the potential of a given level of organization in one system, to explain the variance observed in the other. Such a potential may be cast in mathematical, informational, or physical terms, but for our purpose of physiology–psychology relations, it translates to the idea that the dimensionality of a possibly relevant physiological domain must somehow be matched or correlated to the dimensionality of the mapped object or process in the psychological domain. A physiologist considering construction of relations with domains selected from the unfathomable, rich psychoanalytic language, is expected to suggest an equally rich physiological domain. For instance, a mutated gene (a few-states switch) as a domain corresponding to the rich dynamics of schizo-paranoid personality (or any other complex behavior), would not do; a single gene mutation seems too dull. Likewise, a physiologist arguing that the concept of (for instance) repression is mappable to over-activity of a cluster of neurons positioned somewhere in the brain, would sound dull; this is because one may justly ask: Why repression of this and not that? Why now and not then? Why does this person repress this fact but another does not? Pointing to a locus, in whatever level one chooses to describe the brain, cannot provide answers to such questions. Adopting potential to explain variance as a heuristic in the process of identifying scales for the dialogue does remove quite a few interpretations from the table, but leaves room for many possible choices of interpretations on other, very different levels. So which of these other interpretations would be considered an appropriate, mature choice? This is a phase where personal biases heavily impact on our choices.

The reader is invited to follow my bias and to attempt formation of language relations, a dialogue between concepts derived from relational dynamics of psychological objects and the physiology of representation. In this dialogue between relational psychological objects and physiology, the former constrains and guides the latter in phrasing meaningful questions. The dialogue is offered as a demonstration for the kind of relational alternative to naive reductionism. Let the choice of focusing on relational objects be judged by its capacity to deepen the discourse between psychology and physiology, for "by their fruits ye shall know them, not by their roots."

4 Relational Objects in Psychology

For each individual is the synthesis not only of existing relations, but of the history of these relations. He is the précis of all the past.[1]

From the physiological point of view, establishing a dialogue in the language relation sense begins with interpretation of psychological inferences; that is, incorporating psychoanalytic concepts into the language of physiology. As shown in Chapter 3, the choice of which analytic concept to incorporate, and what physiological entity to map it to, is not dictated by anything within psychological theory or within physiology. It is a creative act.

The concepts of psychoanalysis that I find most interesting to dialogue with are those that concern the organization of experience as a personal historical process; the development of templates of relations between abstract psychological constructs – named "objects" – the identity and coupled dynamics of which define the patterns of an individual's distinct behavior. The relevant cluster of ideas cannot be exclusively attributed to any one psychoanalytic school as it entails a combination of concepts that are present at the heart of classical Freudian psychoanalysis, object relations, self-psychology, and relational and intersubjective theoretical frameworks. To avoid confusion, these are all gathered under the umbrella of one name – relational objects – that will also serve us for the physiological analyses in Chapter 5.

[1] Gramsci (1891–1937), *Selections from the Prison Notebooks of Antonio Gramsci* (1971, p. 353).

Each of the psychological theories that address the relational aspects of objects is itself a complex network of weakly coupled metaphors, allegedly distinct from other schools of psychoanalytic thought. Where should one begin? Which concepts within the language of relational objects in psychology should one choose to interpret into physiology? My initial, naive approach, characteristic of those who are trained in the sciences, was to begin by seeking a definitive textbook, identifying theoretical primitives and attempting to map them to physiology. This is not a trivial path to take; it is perhaps not immediately obvious to regular readers of psychoanalytic texts how different their culture is, in this respect, from that of the sciences; not only in that there are no "definitive textbooks" around, but also that existing canonic texts are not committed to a universal set of conceptual primitives. Moreover, eminent analytic writers aiming at analytic readership invest in interpreting, analyzing, and telling *differences* between schools of thought, rather than focusing on common, agreed-upon, analytic primitives, a natural consequence of a rich *intra*-disciplinary discourse. Furthermore, the very act of reading canonic psychoanalytical texts seriously challenges the physiologist educational–conceptual basis, because the language used literally brings objects to life: objects "love," "identify," "hate," and "reject," they "avoid," "maliciously attack," or "invest" different kinds of "psychic energies" in each other, they may be "frustrated," and so forth. The task is further complicated by references to the loosely defined gross anatomy of the psyche, as well as to the dimension of consciousness, notoriously known for its evasiveness. But persistence pays; after a while the outsider reader begins to acknowledge the indispensability of this free, associative, and anthropomorphic language as a tool to describe the elements of depth psychology.

The following pages are offered as a short description of relational psychological objects as seen through the eyes of a physiologist. Being a naive reader, not fully aware of potentially clannish attitudes among psychoanalytic circles, is a limitation that at times may also be an advantage. Excused as being an observer from the outside, I took the liberty to interpret and sew together a set of ideas that had contributed to the development of relational object theories, regardless of their affiliation with one school or the other. Hence the focus in the following pages on commonalities and their threads, simplified versions of ideas with which physiology may be validated by congruence.

The path begins with a Kleinian concept that seems most intimately related to the world of physiology, continues through Fairbairn's and Ogden's expositions of relations between internal objects, to Bowlby's terminology of control systems, leading to Mitchell's and Stolorow-Atwood's relational and intersubjective frameworks, nested from within and without up to the cultural level. These psychoanalytic writings share an interest in the personal organization of experience in the form of templates of relations between psychological objects; they all assume, implicitly or explicitly, that psychological phenomena can only be understood in the context of object relations. The framework of relational objects in psychology as presented here – while a faint reflection of a whole world of fascinating, labyrinthine discourse – is hopefully rich enough to fertilize the ground wherefrom meaningful neurophysiological questions emerge.

Organization of Relational Objects

It is instructive to begin by considering the psychological realm of the newborn as an internal space that is populated by multiple primitive *phantasies*, a concept developed by Klein and her school. Isaacs, in her exposition of the phantasy concept as understood among Kleinians, describes the phantasy as:

> the mental corollary, the psychic representative, of instinct. There is no impulse, no instinctual urge or response which is not experienced as unconscious phantasy.... The first mental processes, the psychic representatives of bodily impulses and feelings, ... are to be regarded

> as the earliest beginning of phantasies.... All impulses, all feelings, all modes of defense are experienced in phantasies which give them mental life and show their direction and purpose.[2]

Such introduced phantasies are the elementary particles of psychic life, and in their infantile version appear and disappear as immediate consequences of urges and outer circumstances; local in time, not committed to the history of past stimuli or responses, nor to compatibility with each other. "Just as in a dream," says Sussan Isaacs in an article full of style. Hannah Segal further elaborates in her introductory comments to this subject:

> The operation of an instinct... is expressed and represented in mental life by the phantasy of the satisfaction of that instinct by an appropriate object. Since instincts operate from birth, some crudely phantasy life can be assumed as existing from birth.... From the moment the infant starts interacting with the outer world, he is engaged in testing his phantasies in a reality setting.[3]

The origin of the set of primitive phantasies is an issue that Klein and her followers push backward to the hands of physiology, attributing it to "innate knowledge" or "phylogenetic inheritance." For reasons that will become clear at a later point, it is convenient to focus on Segal's phrase "testing his phantasies," and imagine the primitive form of phantasy as a prior hypothesis, evolutionary-based first guess or – in current technological jargon – an IF-THEN procedure (if sensation *X*, then action *Y*). These prior hypotheses, which need be tested, validated, refined, and organized through developmental interaction with the outer world, are primitive in the senses both of (1) being there from birth, and (2) their relation to basic instincts – the somatic drives involved in hunger, thirst, excremental needs, touch, and so forth. Infantile reflexes, such as rooting, sucking, grabbing,

[2] Isaacs (1948, pp. 81–2).
[3] Segal (1975, pp. 13–23).

swimming, stepping, and Moro, may be considered as somatic reflections of these primitive phantasies, proxies for evolutionary-based prior hypotheses about the world.

The initial psychological realm is thus one unified, unconscious inner space, the seat of primitive phantasies that are built to support the most basic needs of the infant by means of prototypic movements, selectively activated by external sensory objects or somatic drives. Primitive phantasies are probably "noisy" – that is, not absolutely silent in the absence of a somatic drive or an external object. They are spontaneously active from time to time, giving rise to prototypic movements with no apparent reason. Such un-entailed movements play an important role in the process of development – as discussed in Chapter 5.

Phantasies are dynamic entities, as one expects hypotheses to be, and they are immediately put to a reality test: "From the moment of birth the infant has to deal with the impact of reality, starting with the experience of the birth itself and proceeding to endless experiences of gratification and frustration of his desires."[4] Reality is not static, nor a look-up table against which the infant may take the time to test his phantasies; reality is the outcome of multiple coupled dynamic processes that are partially impacted by, and depend upon, the infants' movements and behavior. The task of phantasy testing that the infant faces is therefore challenging: convergence to a satisfactory solution – that is, the organization of adaptive, reality-matched links between urges, outer circumstances, and action – is not guaranteed under conditions where hypotheses are tested against a dynamic environment. As can be imagined, this is where the mother's role becomes indispensable. Her body parts are the first major external objects toward which the instincts, the drives, or needs, are directed; the first sensory objects against which the inner world of primitive phantasies may be validated. Fairbairn describes a hypothetical point of entry

[4] Segal (1975, p. 14).

to the process, illuminating the degree of mutual challenge that the infant–mother entity has to address:

> The first … [potentially satisfying] object of the infant is, of course, his mother's breast, although there can be no doubt that the form of his mother as a person soon begins to take shape round the original nucleus of this maternal organ. Under theoretically perfect conditions the … relationship of the infant to his mother would be so satisfactory that a state of … frustration [failure to reduce or satisfy drives] could hardly arise; and, as I see it, there would consequently be no ambivalence on the part of the infant towards his object …[5]

A utopian context is described above, where the activation of phantasies leads to satisfaction of drives, regardless of which movement the infant exercises or what the state of the outer world is. No matter if the infant turns its head to the right or to the left, up or down, a breast is there to satisfy it. No matter what state the external world is in, any time, any place, a breast is there to feed it. The closest condition to this utopia is the intra-uterine environment from which the infant is torn during birth, maybe the most traumatic psycho-physical event in the human life cycle.

I propose to adopt the concept of *symmetry* in characterizing the utopian situation described by Fairbairn. In several domains within the sciences, when a construct is said to be symmetric, the meaning is that the outcome of interacting with the construct is indifferent (invariant) to how one interacts with it. Symmetry must be "broken" to generate uniqueness of responses – that is, to generate sensitivity of the construct to the manner by which it interacts with the world. The beginning of a pot is a symmetric ball of clay; breaking the symmetry of the ball of clay is the process by which endless forms of pottery are created. The first act of symmetry breaking is a major

[5] Fairbairn (1944, p. 82); for didactic purposes the term *libidinal* was omitted and replaced by "[potentially satisfying]," thus reducing the terminological load on physiologically oriented readers.

determinant of future forms by omission of a whole range of potential configurations. Symmetry breaking is a process that governs somatic development, from cell division to organ formation and cellular specialization. As discussed in the pages that follow, symmetry breaking of the inner space may be viewed as the hallmark of mental development, an inevitable process leading to enrichment of the repertoire of the infant's unconscious phantasies (hypotheses) and, eventually, to the adult form of internal mental life and its capacity to adapt. As Isaacs (1948, p. 81) clarifies, phantasies are "... fully active in the normal, no less than in the neurotic mind."

For consistency, the term *primitive phantasy* is reserved to describe a primitive, prior hypothesis – a psychological entity seated in the internal, unconscious space, reflecting an infantile reflex. The term *higher-order phantasy* will be used to refer to forms that evolve from the primitive ones following a process of symmetry breaking. Fairbairn provides an intuition for a (maybe *the*) major symmetry-breaking event and the emergence of higher-order phantasies:

> Such perfect conditions [symmetry] are, however, only theoretically possible for the human infant born into a cultural group; and in actual fact the ... [satisfying] relationship of the infant to his mother is disturbed from the first by a considerable measure of frustration, although, of course, the degree of such frustration varies in different cases.... From the point of view of the infant himself it is a case of his mother becoming an ambivalent object, i.e. an object which is both good and bad. Since it proves intolerable to him to have a good object which is also bad, he seeks to alleviate the situation by splitting the figure of his mother into two objects. Then, in so far as she satisfies him ..., she is a good object, and, in so far as she fails to satisfy him ..., she is a bad object. The situation in which he now finds himself placed proves, however, in its turn to be one which imposes a severe strain upon his capacity for endurance and his power of adjustment.[6]

[6] Fairbairn (1944, p. 82).

Fairbairn stresses the infant's point of view; oblivious to that of the mother and the impacts of "her-self" being a subject, home for her own dynamic mind, a conceptual framework that was later enriched by intersubjective and relational psychoanalytic writers (see below). In Fairbairn's description the perceived external object is the main determinant of the aroused phantasy and the resulting actualization of that phantasy in a movement. Activation of internal representation of a nourishing mother calls for (for example) approaching patterns of behavior (actualization of phantasy). In contrast, activation of representation of an avoiding, retreating mother who pulls her breast away, calls for realization of another phantasy (resulting in, for example, vigorous, seemingly violent, breast biting, thus fastening the feeding maternal object to himself). In other words, one set of sensory stimuli is translated – within the infant's internal psychological space – to a representation that activates a phantasy leading to an apparently approaching behavior. The other set of sensory stimuli is translated within the infant's internal psychological space to a representation that activates another phantasy, leading to an apparently aggressive behavior. Each of these phantasy-activating representations stands for a different aspect of the external object, the good and the bad mother. The two aspects cannot be too different in their physical shape, because the spatial features involved, associated with the mother figure, are physically similar in both cases. But they are psychologically very different, hence the ambivalence Fairbairn describes: the same external physical entity (mother) transformed into two very different psychological entities.

This idea of good and bad mother is traceable back into ancient times, as nicely illustrated in molded clay breasts encysted with (for example) vulture beaks, decorating the "shrines" of *Çatalhöyük*, a ca. 7000 B.C. settlement in Anatolia; "the carnivore mouth (food-consuming) inside the lactating nipple (food-providing)" as phrased by Gifford-Gonzalez in an accessible account (On beasts in breasts) of this fascinating topic.[7] Also,

[7] Gifford-Gonzalez (2007, p. 99).

the same idea is captured in the concept of "the loving and the terrible mother" archetype in Jung's writings, albeit from a societal–cultural point of view, adding an interesting dimension to the discussion.[8]

The caricature I have in mind when trying to intuit the ambivalence described by Fairbairn is akin to the case of bi-stable perception, mainspring of much interest in cognitive and simple human behavior studies. A famous example that caters to a very limited control on what is perceived in ambivalent settings is shown in Figure 4.1, a picture named *My wife and my mother-in-law.* Our perception switches between seeing a young, attractive girl and an old unsightly woman. We cannot see them both simultaneously. The observer might enforce some control, attempting fixating on one interpretation of the figure, but it does not hold for long. For the infant, of course, the situation is far from being a matter of scientific or cognitive curiosity; experiencing a providing, life-sustaining object as ambiguous (inconsistent) is a major source of discontent, challenging satisfaction of basic needs, calling for a functional resolution by symmetry breaking within the inner space. Fairbairn describes the resolution that object relations theory proposes:

> Being a situation in outer reality, it is one which he finds himself impotent to control, and which, accordingly, he seeks to mitigate by such means as are at his disposal. The means at his disposal are limited; and the technique which he adopts is more or less dictated by this limitation. He accordingly follows the only path open to him and, since outer reality seems unyielding, he does his best to transfer ... the situation to the field of inner reality, within which he feels situations to be more under his own control.[9]

8 Jung (1972, p. 16).

9 Fairbairn (1944, pp. 82–3). A note for the psychologically educated reader: The words "the traumatic factor in," which some might consider critical, were omitted as they point to a distinction between Klein and Fairbairn on the issue of which aspect of the object is transferred to the inner world: "[I] disagree ... with his [Fairbairn's] view that to begin with only the bad object is internalized ..." (Melanie Klein, Notes on some schizoid mechanisms [1975, p. 3]). Klein's version is more congruent with the present essay, although for our dialogue the choice does not matter much.

Figure 4.1. Hill, W. E. (William Ely), 1887–1962, artist.
Date Published: 1915 November 6. Public domain. http://www.loc.gov/pictures/item/2010652001/

This is the symmetry-breaking machinery postulated by object-relations theorists. The resolution of the ambivalent situation "which imposes a severe strain upon his [the infant's] capacity for endurance and his power of adjustment," involves representation of the two conflicting aspects of the ambiguous object as two separate entities in an internal unconscious space, giving rise to two separate internal objects. Having two different internal objects allows the infant to elaborate and refine the primitive phantasies by formation of new higher-order phantasies that properly and selectively relate to each of these apparently conflicting aspects that are manifested in the one physical mother. Metaphorically, the one figure of the young–old female is internally represented as two distorted cut-out aspects (Figure 4.2), each serving in separation as an object to relate to. It follows that there must be features in the external object that cater to the classification that the infant needs to exercise in telling which mother he perceives at any given time – the nourishing or the retreating; maybe a gesture, or a tone of voice, something that is unique to the one percept but not to the other. In the absence of such features that enable classification, that is, the cases of impervious or unpredicted mother, a door leading to psychopathology is left wide open.

The picture that emerges is of an abstract inner unconscious space that begins at birth (or maybe earlier) as one whole integral home for primitive phantasies, prior hypotheses about sensory-motor relations that optimize satisfaction of somatic drives. Reality forces this space to split up, giving rise to internal objects (representations of different aspects of the external object) that selectively activate unconscious higher-order phantasies (elaborated hypotheses), leading in turn to suitable movements.

This picture does not constitute a major departure from processes that Freud (Figure 4.3) described in his writings, processes that entail splitting of the internal space to representations of aspects of external objects, representations that may even replace the role of the external objects in shaping behavior and external relations.[10] Freud specifically talks about splitting that enables "mental life" to maintain two

10 Freud (1917, pp. 237–58).

Figure 4.2. Two different aspects of the ambivalent figure.
Hill, W. E. (William Ely), 1887–1962, artist; Date Published: 1915 November 6. Public domain. http://www.loc.gov/pictures/item/2010652001/

contradictory "attitudes" toward reality "side by side."[11] He opens his 1938 paper on "Splitting of the Ego in the Process of Defence," referring (with an unmistakable style) to the process of splitting and its functional role:[12]

> I find myself for a moment in the interesting position of not knowing whether what I have to say should be regarded as something long familiar and obvious or as something entirely new and puzzling.... Let us suppose, then, that a child's ego [internal space] is under the sway of a powerful instinctual demand which it is

11 Freud (1927, p. 156).

12 Freud (1938, pp. 275–6); with text in [square brackets] added for didactic purposes.

Figure 4.3. A portrait of Sigmund Freud, 1909 (by Max Halberstadt. From http://commons.wikimedia.org/wiki/File:Sigmund_Freud_by_Max_Halberstadt_1909_cph.3c33801.jpg).

accustomed to satisfy and that it is suddenly frightened by an experience which teaches it that the continuance of this satisfaction will result in an almost intolerable real danger. It must now decide either to recognize the real danger, give way to it and renounce the instinctual satisfaction, or to disavow reality and make itself believe that there is no reason for fear, so that it may

> be able to retain the satisfaction. Thus there is a conflict between the demand by the instinct and the prohibition by reality [Segal's "impacts of reality"]. But in fact the child takes neither course, or rather he takes both simultaneously, which comes to the same thing. He replies to the conflict with two contrary reactions, both of which are valid and effective. On the one hand, with the help of certain mechanisms he rejects reality and refuses to accept any prohibition; on the other hand, in the same breath he recognizes the danger of reality, takes over the fear of that danger as a pathological symptom and tries subsequently to divest himself of the fear.... Both of the parties to the dispute obtain their share: the instinct is allowed to retain its satisfaction and proper respect is shown to reality. But everything has to be paid for in one way or another, and this success is achieved at the price of a rift in the ego which never heals but which increases as time goes on. The two contrary reactions to the conflict persist as the centre-point of a splitting of the ego.

In the above excerpt, liberty was taken to translate the term *ego* to the term *internal space*. This is not the place to elaborate on the history of its usage, for, like other basic concepts in psychoanalysis, the concept of ego has many facets and refuses to be too narrowly defined. It is maybe convenient to conceive the ego – this internal space – as being the home for a spectrum of phantasies (primitive and higher-order), ranging from the most hidden, completely unconscious, to more conscious processes of sensing–representation–action.

While, clearly, the footsteps of relations between internal objects are traceable back to Freud's writings, it is the integrated contributions of Klein, Isaacs, Segal, Fairbairn, Kohut, Bion, Winnicott, and many other thinkers that solidified the two tenets of object relations theory, namely: (1) the clinical observation of identification and transference entail rich and dynamic intra-personal relations between objects, and (2) that these internal relations are reflected in (and determinants of) interpersonal relations. Thomas Ogden purified these ideas in his beautiful analysis of the concept of internal object relations,[13] arriving at the inevitable conclusion that the process of symmetry breaking within the internal space is much more than evolving internal representations of the external objects:

> An internal object relationship necessarily involves an interaction between two subdivisions of the personality, each subdivision capable of being an active psychological agency.... I suggest that the internalization of an object relationship be thought of as necessarily involving a dual subdivision of the ego. *Such a dual split would result in the formation of two new suborganizations of the ego, one identified with the self in the external object relationship and the other thoroughly identified with the object.*[14]

It is instructive to assume that the scheme of internal object relations involves representation of the pattern of external relations as a whole; a complex that includes: (1) *A self component of the relationship* – this is the representation of the self that is in relations with the relevant aspect of the external object. For instance, the satisfied self that is in relations with the nourishing mother; or, alternatively, the vigorous, seemingly violent self that is in relations with the avoiding or retreating mother; (2) *A representation of the relevant aspect of the external object* – for instance, the good internal mother object or the bad internal mother object; and (3) *the relations between these two components.* Ogden believes that this kind of object internalization can occur only in early development, and involves poorly differentiated identifications, where one "is becoming the object."[15] Adult internalizations are more subtle, "built upon existing splits ... and do not involve the creation of new ones," says Ogden,[16] echoing

13 Ogden (1983, 1986).
14 Ogden (1983, pp. 233–4).
15 Ogden (1986, p. 150).
16 Ogden (1983, p. 234).

Freud's assertion that this primal "rift in the ego … never heals but increases as time goes on."[17]

Thus, the basic form of internal object relations includes a pair of components, a "self" component and an "other" component. The ambivalent mother object gives rise to two such pairs, reflecting good and bad mothers and the corresponding selves. Each one of these pairs is in relations within itself, and with the real external object. With this scheme in mind, fundamental analytic concepts may be defined, including *transference* (experiencing an external subject as an internal object) and *projective identification* (the process whereby the external subject literally takes the role of the said internal object in the relationships).

Considering external subjects as well as internal objects as active psycho-*logical* agencies – that is, systems conforming to some degree of generative relations – it is tempting to reflect back now on our description of language (model) relations, and contemplate the apparent parallelism. This parallelism is acknowledged in psychoanalytic circles, at least among those versed in systems and control theory. Here are the words of John Bowlby to that effect: "Each individual builds working models of the world and of himself in it, with the aid of which he perceives events, forecasts the future, and constructs his plans."[18] The elements of these working models are internal object relations, namely representations of self and world, as well as related higher-order phantasies (Bowlby's "plans"). Bowlby stresses the complex and dynamic nature of the environment, and the need to elaborate internal models that are "becoming increasingly sophisticated, in particular by their coming to incorporate representational models of the environment and important people in it and also of the self as a living active person."[19] Under these circumstances, the possibility

[17] Freud (1938, p. 276).
[18] Bowlby (1973, p. 203). This is literally a description of Rosen's relations between structured languages (or models) as discussed in Chapter 3.
[19] Bowlby (1988, p. 62).

of wild interpretation and incomplete validation by congruence offers a perspective toward psychopathology: "the patterns of interaction to which the models lead, having become habitual, generalized, and largely unconscious, persist in more or less uncorrected and unchanged state even when the individual in later life is dealing with persons who treat him in ways entirely unlike those that his parents adopted when he was a child."[20] Bowlby's perceptive comments capture the essence of internal object relations, from which he and his colleagues derived the principles of attachment theory.[21]

As mentioned above, the primal split involves poorly differentiated identifications ("becoming the object")[22] and occurs during infantile stages in response to ambiguous relations with the basic object (mother or equivalent). This split, or "rift … which never heals" as Freud called it, is the first symmetry breaking and, being first, dramatically impacts on later life splits that – according to Ogden – are "built upon existing splits … and do not involve creation of new ones." This does not contradict the above idea expressed by Bowlby about multiple representations of environment and selves. We may assume, at least for the purpose of our present discussion on relational objects, that later splits (representations and relations among them, or Bowlby's models) are nested within the primal split. In other words, there can be many different "increasingly sophisticated" aspects to the primitive "self" and "other" components of object relations. Different psychoanalytic writers treat the entailed concept of multiple selves differently. The subject matter is elegantly summarized in *Hope and Dread in Psychoanalysis*, written by Stephen A. Mitchell, a prominent voice in establishing the concept of self (selves) in relation to others,[23] and one of the leading figures

20 Bowlby (1988, p. 130).
21 "Historically, attachment theory was developed as a variant of object-relations theory." Ibid., p. 29.
22 Ogden (1986, p. 150).
23 Mitchell (1993).

in the acknowledgment of *relationality*, a critical concept that travels throughout this essay in many layers simultaneously.

It is obvious, reading the texts referenced above (Freud and Klein, Isaacs, Fairbairn, Winnicott, Bowlby, Ogden, and others), that relations *in the real*, especially at very early stages of development but also in later life, are reflected in relations between objects in the internal psychic space. Psychoanalysis, from its inception – and more so in the way it was promoted in the British schools of thought – seriously takes the relations with real others as determinants in the organization of experience as a personal historical process. The focus of these writers, however, was on the relational dynamics between internal objects as reflected in the relations to the real other. The presence of that *real other as a subject* having an internal psychic space, housing relational dynamics between internal objects, and the entailed coupled dynamics between the two subjects, were left – to use Mitchell's phrase – bracketed for decades, but not unacknowledged. Many different factors gave rise to such bracketing of the intersubjective perspective, ranging from social and political forces within and outside the discipline, through the natural and gradual evolution of a discipline, to different epistemological stances toward the study of the mind.[24] Whatever these reasons are, déjà vu is experienced when the developmental timeline of psychology in general, and psychoanalysis in particular, is reviewed. The development of psychoanalytic theory is itself a process of symmetry breaking that echoes the development of the internal psychic space of the individual, starting from the omnipotent, symmetric, and self-contained Freudian framework, going through a series of symmetry-breaking splits that are inevitable when facing the challenges of interaction with the real world, thus making space for conceptual frameworks that – like Bowlby's internal models – are "becoming increasingly sophisticated, in particular by their coming

[24] Aron (1996); Mitchell (2000).

to incorporate representational models of the environment."[25] Déjà vu is also experienced in the sense of the frustration, underlying the primal split, echoed in the split between the structural and functional psychology around the transition from the nineteenth to the twentieth century, as well as in the split between classical Freudians and the relational-intersubjective movement of psychoanalysis. It is illuminating to read Dewey's 1896 seminal paper on the erroneous generalization of the reflex arc concept in psychology, with the emergence of relational psychology in mind; even more so when one considers the geographical distributions of these structural (largely European) and functional (largely American) psychological frameworks.

What Stolorow and Atwood wisely named in their exposition of the intersubjective perspective "the myth of the isolated individual mind"[26] is now widely accepted. Rephrasing Winnicott – there is no such thing as a mind of an individual in isolation from its relations to the minds of others, and without those other minds there would be no individual. As repeatedly stated by Atwood and Stolorow, Mitchell, Aron, and other relational psychologists, a major consequence of this acceptance is that *understanding a psychological phenomenon inevitably entails understanding its intersubjective context*. This has implications for neurophysiology, as it is an attack on naive reductionism.

I opened this chapter with a comment on the very act of reading canonic psychoanalytical texts, an act that seriously challenges the physiologist educational and conceptual basis because the language used literally brings internal objects to life: objects "love," "identify," "hate," "reject," "avoid," may be "frustrated," and so forth. Indeed, at first sight this all sounds a rather shaky language for the scientifically minded. But the use of such language does have scientific grounds, although a measure of imagination is (admittedly) required for that. In a paper titled "Adaptation and regulation with

25 Bowlby (1988, p. 62).
26 Stolorow and Atwood (1992).

signal detection implies internal model," Eduardo Sontag provides a proof of an internal model theorem:[27] under reasonable mathematical assumptions, a system that adapts to a class of external signals must necessarily contain (within in it, so to speak) a subsystem which is capable of generating the signals to which it is adapted. In a continuation paper[28] this result is generalized to incomplete adaptation.[29] While acknowledging the gap between mathematical and psychological languages, perceiving the psychological inner space as being populated by agents that are capable of generating the external signals to which they have adapted in the past is, after all, an idea that the scientifically minded can contemplate.

Primitives to Dialogue With

We conclude our attempt to portray a simplified version of the framework of relational objects in psychology, by pointing to primitives whose echoes we intend to seek in the physiological domain. The *inner space*, mostly distant from awareness, often referred to as ego, is the seat of phantasies. The inner space is *reflexive*, characterized by self-engaging dynamism of interpretation and projection among its internal objects, a dynamism that is sensitive – within limits – to external events. At birth this inner space is occupied by infantile reflexes (primitive phantasies) that, when triggered by environmental cues (stimuli), satisfy basic instincts. The concept of *primal symmetry* of the inner space is offered as a reference to a utopian situation where

27 Sontag (2003).

28 Andrews, Sontag and Iglesias (2008).

29 A note to the mathematically-oriented reader: Francis and Wonham introduced the internal model theorem under more restrictive assumptions in the 1970s ("The internal model principle for linear multivariable regulators," *Applied Mathematics & Optimization*, 1975, and a series of follow-up studies) for the case of a linear system. Sontag generalized the result by proving the theorem for the case of a non-linear system that is not a priori split to modules, and does not require the adaptation to be perfect.

all the instinctual needs are provided by means of the environment (mother) and infantile reflexes. *Discontent* is the psychological consequence of an ambivalent environment, a situation in which similar external objects call for the activation of very different (often contradicting) phantasies. It is an unavoidable consequence of the caregiver being a subject, home for her own internal object relations. The term *symmetry breaking* is offered as a reference to the process of splitting the psychological inner space to fit the contradicting demands of the environment. Hence, discontent leads to changes in the structure of the psychological inner space, giving rise to symmetry breaking and the emergence of *internal objects*. The concept of *internal object relations* refers to the interactions between representations (of selves and others), within and across split-offs. The content of – and the relations between – internal objects are *adaptive* to a degree that determines the potential outcome of *intersubjective contexts* within which our psychical and physical lives are embedded. Hence, all these entities and all these processes are at the service of the organization of experience as a personal historical process: the development of templates of relations between internal objects, which are exposed in later relational, intersubjective settings.

We turn now to the physiological codomain, contemplating ideas that partially correspond to the above primitives of psychological relational objects. The hope is to succeed in presenting a physiological perspective that evokes a feeling of reflecting on relational psychological objects in a new language, lending itself to language relations of the kind described in Chapter 3.

5 Reflections on Relational Physiology

Structure ceases to be an external force which crushes man, assimilates him to itself and makes him passive, and is transformed into a means of freedom ...[1]

Influenced by the communist philosophy of his time, Lev Semyonovich Vygotsky (1896–1934) was probably the clearest among the early scholars calling for analysis of human "higher" psychological functions in the context of individual and societal historical–cultural development.[2] He saw the psychological development of humans as part of the general historical development of our species, and must be understood as such. Vygotsky insisted that we should free ourselves from the dominance of the stimulus–response paradigm, according to which the relations between humans and nature are viewed as unidirectional, "the assumption that only nature affects human beings and only natural conditions determine historical development."[3] He reasoned, following Engels' dialectical approach, that human behavior has a transforming effect on nature – by means of the development of tools – which in turn impacts on how nature is experienced by humans and changes them.[4] Hence, human behavior

1 Gramsci (1971, p. 367).
2 Vygotsky (1978), an edited collection of his essays.
3 Ibid. (p. 60).
4 Vygotsky (and Engels) would have embraced every word in Garry Kasparov's (2010) commentary on the impacts of chess computer programs on the style of present-day chess players (described in the section on reverse engineering).

as experienced at any given point in time is the result of an evolving complex of coupled dynamics, a dialectical process that spans a wide range of time scales, and can only be understood through its phylogenetic and ontogenetic developmental timeline by "analyzing processes, not objects."[5]

Over the past several decades, Vygotsky's vision has been realized within the disciplines of comparative anatomy, zooarchaeology, and paleoanthropology. As shown below,[6] the rich data and theoretical insights offered in these disciplines – incorporating broad evolutionary and cultural perspectives – are most relevant as a means to bridge the relational psychological framework to neurophysiological research.[7]

Evolution of the Relational Brain

The modern human (*Homo sapiens*) is a member of the Hominidae family, other members being the orangutans, gorillas, and chimpanzees.[8] Fossil remains indicate that the earliest hominins existed in Africa six or seven million years ago. The most familiar early hominin genus, *Australopithecus*, existed from at least four million years ago, and survived approximately two million years. Phillip V. Tobias (Tobias 1981), in telling the story of the emergence of humanity describes these early hominins (*Australopithecus africanus*) as upright-walking creatures, having teeth smaller than those of African apes, but a similar brain size. Estimates of the adult brain volume of

5 Ibid. (p. 61).

6 The general approach offered here is much inspired by the work of John C. Eccles in his book *Evolution of the Brain: Creation of the Self* (1989).

7 Two excellent and accessible books written by a leading evolutionary anthropologist – Michael Tomasello – *The Cultural Origins of Human Cognition* (1999) and *A Natural History of Human Thinking* (2014), offer a broad and updated view of cultural impacts on human cognition.

8 Lewin and Foley (2004, pp. 210–12) classification.

early hominins average around 450 ml, which is approximately the volume of the modern chimpanzee brain. Since then – over four million years of evolution – the human brain volume has expanded three-fold.[9] Most of this exceptionally fast expansion of the human brain volume has occurred over the last two million years, which also saw the emergence of geographical range extension and continuing elaboration of culture and technology.

Several observations indicate that there might be a connection between the evolutionary expansion of the brain and the relational nature of human behavior. One of these observations concerns the extent of brain growth during the first years of individual development. The size of the adult human brain is four times larger compared to its size at birth. This four-fold brain growth takes place over the first five years of development,[10] spanning infancy, toddlerhood, and the exploratory (pre-school) age. These numbers are different from those of the apes: the brain size in the adult ape is about twice its size at birth, and in the baby chimpanzee – our closest relative – brain size maturation takes place within the first two years, with marginal addition in the third year. Thus the human embryo, after being forced to leave the protective environment of the uterus, goes through most brain developmental stages outside. This means that for quite a significant period after giving birth the mother is an extension of her uterus; the baby-born is not viable without her. As such, Winnicott's famous aphorism is a physiological truism.[11]

While *in utero*, the embryo exists within a symmetric environment where all needs are continuously provided, controlled, and precisely matched by maternal physiological systems, mostly detached from

9 The average volume of the modern human brain is approximately 1350 ml.
10 Foley and Lee (1991).
11 Winnicott (1960, footnote number 4, p. 586): "[T]here is no such thing as an infant … whenever one finds an infant one finds maternal care, and without maternal care there would be no infant."

the mother's subjective existence.[12] Once outside, the context is qualitatively different, as interactions with a *mother subject* are entailed. Being directly exposed to (and impacted by) the conflicting demands of the environment on a subjective caregiver during development, the baby has to negotiate the fulfillment of its basic needs with a physiologically and psychologically complex mother subject, as its brain expands four-fold.

From this point of view, the human brain, during most of its developmental timeline and most of its physical growth, must handle – in a manner of speaking – relations with a subject whose behavior is dictated by her internal psychological space, object relations, and intersubjective contexts. To the extent that the effective structure and dynamics of the brain reflect the history of its activity, the brain thus becomes inherently relational. This conclusion is congruent with comparisons made by primatologists studying evolution of brains and social behavior in chimpanzees and humans. Even though the developmental timeline of chimpanzees is very close to ours, they seem to differ in their capacity to relate. For instance, by monitoring gaze direction in complex scenes, it is possible to demonstrate convincingly that chimpanzees focus their attention on salient objects; this is in contrast to human babies, who always relate to objects and scenes within social contexts, directing their attention to people who act as agents.[13] Such differences make sense when the fact of the human brain's development in a seemingly more relational context is fully acknowledged.

12 Cases of maternal physiological effects due to maternal mental states are ignored at this stage of our discussion, although such effects are undoubtedly relevant in the wider context.

13 Matsuzawa (2013). See Myowa-Yamakoshi, Scola, and Hirata (2012) for an interesting study that demonstrates how human babies, unlike chimpanzees, attend to faces of subjects in action, whereas chimpanzees focus on the actions of a subject and do not attend preferentially to the face.

Allometric studies that correlate cortex dimensions to social interactions and language further enrich the view on relational aspects as reflected in the anatomy and development of the brain. In primates, the ratio of brain to body size is exceptionally high, but paleoanthropological data suggest that it is a mistake to treat the brain as a whole in relating its size to behavioral evolution. The brain is built of different structures that are clearly visible – even to the naked eye. Among these, the rate of growth of the cortex over the last two million years is steeper in comparison to rates of growth of other structures.[14] Taken together with the fact that the cortex constitutes more than 70% of the human brain volume[15] (in contrast to, for instance, 30% in the rat),[16] it has become an object of numerous studies, aiming to identify it as *the* seat of qualities that underlay the anthropocentric *scala naturae.* Unfortunately for those who try to promote an anthropocentric view of nature, attempts to establish correlations between various indices of cortical dimensions and general cognitive or sensory motor skills, are not very convincing.[17] Since the early 1990s, however, a different approach toward the relations between cortical measures and behavioral capacities has taken over, which seems right to the point from the perspective of relational psychological objects; it is known in the discipline of paleoanthropology as the "social brain hypothesis."

In reviewing the concept of the social brain, Dunbar[18] describes different indices of social complexity and social skills that are shown to correlate with the volume of the primate cortex. Among these, social group size correlates significantly with the absolute cortex volume. The studies of Dunbar and his colleagues put forward an

14 Finlay, Darlington, and Nicastro (2001).

15 Numbers vary between different reports, but remain within the same ballpark. See, for instance, a review article "How many neurons do you have? Some dogmas of quantitative neuroscience under revision" by Lent et al. (2012).

16 Swanson (1995).

17 Butler and Hodos (2005, pp. 100–9).

18 Dunbar (2003).

interesting argument that links bonding interactions among members of one's group to cortex size and the evolution of language. Consider social grooming – the activity of one individual maintaining the body of another individual in a group. In social animals, grooming serves as means to establish relationships. It turns out that among nonhuman primates, there is an impressive statistical correlation between cortex size, the number of individuals that the animal is in relations with, and the time spent on social grooming.[19] To the extent that one is willing to accept time spent on social grooming as an index for relationality (not a trivial entailment), encephalization – that is, the disproportionate growth of brain in general and the relative increase in the cortex in particular – is correlated with being relational. Dunbar and his co-workers further argue that since the time required for social grooming in group sizes that characterize humans would be much too long to be realized under reasonable constraints, more efficient means for expression of relations need to be evolved.[20] This brought the proponents of the social brain hypothesis to point to the development of language as an alternative, more efficient means for social bonding within and between large human groups: "pressure for larger groups seems to be the driving factor behind the evolution of human language and all of the cultural manifestations associated with it."[21] The

19 Aiello and Dunbar (1993).

20 Human group size is estimated to be in the order of 100 subjects, real ones – in contrast to virtual, computer-based social network relations; see, for instance, Hill and Dunbar (2003). Note that in a hierarchical organization the large group size need not impact on the number of related-to individuals; consider the extreme case of linear hierarchy, where each member is serving one individual above, and being served by one individual below, in which case the group size does not impact on social grooming time. But hunter–gatherer human groups have an egalitarian ethos, characterized by a suppressed hierarchical structure; such groups provided the social context for the human brain evolution. See, for instance, Fehr, Bernhard, and Rockenbach (2008); Jensen, Hare, Call and Tomasello (2006), and references therein.

21 Aiello and Dunbar (1993); Dunbar (2003).

emergence of language – so viewed – is an outcome of a basic need to relate.

The discussion so far focuses on the brain. But one should keep in mind that the alleged pressure to relate to each other is reflected in the evolution of physical structures other than the brain. For instance, among the great apes the sclera is white only in humans. White sclera makes the eyes especially visible. Tomasello and his colleagues suggested that this recently evolved anatomical feature is a means to enhance the capacity of humans to socially interact by following the gaze of the other.[22] They have shown that human infants (but not chimpanzees, gorillas and bonobos) heavily rely on the direction of the other's gaze in non-verbal communication. Such theoretical arguments and empirical data, pointing to expressions of relational aspects in structures *outside* the brain, surface the issue of brain localization, and resonates with relationality and intersubjectivity in psychology. Leslie Brothers[23] provides an impressive range of arguments showing how much we (physiologists and psychologists) might be missing by adhering to the *fallacy of the lonesome brain idea*, echoing Atwood and Stolorow's stance toward the myth of the isolated mind.[24] Brothers named her book *Friday's Footprint*, using the image of Robinson Crusoe as a metaphor for the impossibility of the isolated, self-contained brain as conceived by many (but not all) contemporary neuroscientists. The mind, says Brothers, is not a private system; it is a public system of signs and behaviors. Our tendency to conflate concepts that belong to the public language of mind (a *process*) with coordinates of *objects* in the private brain is a category error. To me, the story of the white sclera, alongside the unique anatomy of the human vocal apparatus, is a beautiful reminder of that effect; both are *outside* the brain. Following up on Brothers' arguments, searching

[22] Tomasello et al. (2007).
[23] Brothers (1997).
[24] Stolorow and Atwood (1992).

for the coordinates of a complex psychological process in the brain is analogous to a potter searching for a shape of a mug in raw clay; the latter may be used to create one, and the potter's imagination is undeniably helpful here, but there is no mug in the raw material. This is the kind of fallacy that Vygotsky meant to avoid in his call for analyzing processes rather than objects.[25]

The paleoanthropological, primatological, and comparative neuroanatomical arguments, of which only a small sample was described here, by the very nature of the data they are based on, are not free of cracks. Yet taken together, they support the assertion that the relational context is a powerful determinant of human physiological evolution. More to the point from the perspective of the present text, encephalization, the disproportionate development of the cerebral hemispheres, is tied to the development of human relational capacities. This is not to say that the relational capacity is seated here or there in the brain, as explained in the following discussion on the difficulties inherent in attempts to localize behavioral traits.

Localization, in the Gross

> *We have learnt from the localizationists that the cerebral cortex is responsible for the highest psychic functions, but we do not know what to make of this in view of the stupendous cerebral cortex of a cow, which most nonspecialists can hardly distinguish from that of man.*[26]

The above ideas and data on the evolution of the cerebral hemispheres join a host of well-established clinical neurology facts that link cortical physiology and pathology with cognitive and emotional phenomena in health and disease. Consider, for instance, the effects of cortical lesions, seizures, and corpus callosotomy (split brain studies), the impacts of focal and global electrical or chemical

[25] Vygotsky (1978) p. 61.
[26] Braitenberg (1977[1973], p. 101).

perturbations, strong correlations between complex behavioral phenomena and activation of unique cortical areas, and in more recent years the captivating settings of brain interfaces that translate cortical activity to commands that control machines "by thought." The data are so appealing that neuroscientists tend to localize within the cerebral cortex the cognitive superiority of man over all other animate life. Statements such as "the cerebral cortex is concerned with cognitive functioning"[27] abound. Serious attempts are being made to identify the cortical loci (or, in a softer version, the neural correlate) of a wide range of phenomena and epiphenomena, from human consciousness through psychological transference to religious and non-religious beliefs. This is part of a larger trend to formulate brain anatomy and function in terms borrowed from classical engineering, where functions are identified with tangible parts.[28] But things are not that simple; a comment on the naive version of localization is wanted, before contemplating the challenge of seeking an alternative.

The tendency to identify brain parts with behavioral functions is not new. Its primitive version – generally referred to as phrenology – flourished in the transition from the eighteenth century into the nineteenth century, and constituted a cluster of ideas about relations between human traits and various physical measures of head dimensions. Modern versions of phrenology use less trivial measures, focusing more on brain activation as revealed by application of sophisticated imaging technologies. Much care must be exercised in interpreting the data of such function localization projects. It is immediately clear that when complex systems and their relations with the environment are considered – especially systems that are

[27] A subtitle of a section on the cortex in a chapter dedicated to the anatomical organization of the nervous system, in: Kandel, Schwartz, and Jessell (2000, p. 324), a major textbook of the discipline.

[28] The qualification "classical" is in place because other kinds of engineering exist, albeit advanced and less familiar to the uninformed reader, where functions cannot be identified with parts.

inherently heterarchical – it might be meaningless to localize general concepts such as transference, love, cognition, and consciousness. This is well-acknowledged by most serious practicing neurophysiologists, as reflected in the qualifying terminology that accompanies their reports in professional scientific texts (less so in reports appealing to the layperson and docile benefactors). Attempts to flatten the complex dynamical and heterarchical nature of brain activity, which is practically inseparable from the dynamics of the environment, lead to vague statements about brain areas that are "involved in," "associated with," "play a key role," and so forth. Blurring scientific reports by use of such qualifiers does not really promote our understanding of the complexity involved. The four wheels of my car play a key role in, are involved in, or are associated with the fact that the car may move me around, at will, from one place to another. If the wheels are removed (a "lesion" experiment) the car cannot move; moreover, the correlation between movement of these wheels and the trajectory of the car in space is no less than perfect. But no one would use these facts to localize the moving capacity of the car to wheels. Rather, it is in the way things are connected, relate, and interact with each other and with the world that matter. This idea is well established in neuropsychology, and its seeds are traceable to the founding text of psychoanalysis, Freud's *Interpretation of Dreams* published in 1900: "ideas, thoughts, and psychic formations in general must not in any case be localized in organic elements of the nervous system but, so to speak, *between them*, where resistances and association tracks form the correlate corresponding to them. Everything that can become an object of internal perception is *virtual*, like the image in the telescope produced by the crossing of light-rays."[29]

Debates concerning the meaning of localizing behavioral features in the brain have been maintained as relevant to varying degrees over

[29] Freud (1995[1938], p. 509).

many years.[30] As pointed out by Flugel in his lively account (published 80 years ago) *A Hundred Years of Psychology, 1833–1933*:

> [T]here seems to be a cycle of fashions with regard to this question of localization. In the days before phrenology, there was little if any suggestion of a precise localization of functions. The phrenologists at one step introduced localization of a highly specific order. Flourens,[31] though his own work proved localization of a kind (a very different kind from that of the phrenologists), yet maintained that the brain functioned as a whole. His work was in a sense a compromise – 'localization in the gross, but not in the fine.' Some fifty years later [that is, 1870s], when the 'new phrenology' was ushered in by the introduction of fresh techniques in the investigation of the brain, the search for centers corresponding to specific functions once again became the guiding principle and remained so for the last quarter of the nineteenth century. In recent years the work of Franz and Lashley in experimental neurology, and of the 'Gestalt' and 'Factor'[32] schools in pure psychology has again emphasized the importance of the more quantitative aspects of brain function as a whole.[33]

John Carl Flugel, an English analyst, died in 1955 and did not have the chance to observe the present rebound of localization.

This holistic–localist issue goes beyond brain research, reflected (for instance) in present-day heated dialogues between reductionist geneticists who unabashedly declare the organism to be a product fully defined by DNA sequences on the one hand, and system theorists who argue for inseparability of biological phenomena from their environmental contexts, on the other;[34] the age old nature–nurture debate. In

30 A concise historical review of this subject appears in Stanley Finger's *Origins of Neuroscience* (1994, pp. 32–61).

31 Jean Pierre Flourens (1794–1867), a French physiologist who conducted a meticulous series of ablation studies in pigeons in the 1820s, aiming to validate phrenology.

32 This is – by and large – Spearman's approach (formalized based on the statistical applications to psychology), which attributes human intelligence to interaction between two factors, generalized and task-specific.

33 Flugel (1934, pp. 53–4).

34 Noble (2006).

their essence, the conflicts are about the relative contributions of structure and dynamics in shaping the functional capacities of living systems. These debates are fueled – to philosophers' delight – by category errors and inopportune manners of speaking. It is true that biological structure is not completely impenetrable to localization; when the brain is stimulated or lesioned in different loci, different functional consequences are entailed. Similarly, a point mutation of a gene may cause a well-defined macroscopic phenomenology (recall the cystic fibrosis example discussed in Chapter 2). However, as repeatedly stated over the past 100 years, there is a sharp difference of category between identifying a local cause of a given *symptom* and localizing a *function*. The impacts of the entailed category error are further amplified when combined with scientific research programs that confuse clinically applied objectives with formal understanding. Luckily, when stressed by a critical reviewer, the more serious representatives of the parties involved in this Babylonian *confusio linguarum* are closer to each other than one would think when relying solely on their manner of speaking.

I base my stance regarding the subject of structure versus dynamism on well-documented data demonstrating reorganization of localization following behavioral experience or damage to the nervous system in general and the cortex in particular. These reorganizations may occur throughout life and include significant changes in the place and shape of cortical activities that correlate with well-defined symptoms and behaviors, changes that are dictated by the nature of the interaction with the environment.[35] When environmental changes entail new patterns of interaction between our sensory–motor envelope and the ambience, substantial modifications are observed in both the positions and shapes of cortical areas that are said to correlate with the relevant behavior. Viewed from the basic science angle – that is, from the perspective of gaining formal understanding – large-scale cortical plasticity implies that *localization is not an explanation* of

[35] For example, Buonomano and Merzenich (1998); Xerri (2012).

the functioning of the brain; rather *localization and its dynamism are things to be explained* by brain science. James, in reference to the tendency of pointing to a given brain area as the seat of this or that behavioral feature, says that:

> Phrenology hardly does more than restate the problem. To answer the question, "Why do I like children?" by saying, "Because you have a large organ of philoprogenitiveness," but renames the phenomenon to be explained. What is my philoprogenitiveness? Of what mental elements does it consist? And how can a part of the brain be its organ? A science of the mind must reduce such complex manifestations as 'philoprogenitiveness' to their elements. A science of the brain must point out the functions of its elements. A science of the relations of mind and brain must show how the elementary ingredients of the former correspond to the elementary functions of the latter. But phrenology, except by occasional coincidence, takes no account of elements at all. Its 'faculties,' as a rule, are fully equipped persons in a particular mental attitude.... A portion of the brain competent to be the adequate seat of such a faculty would needs be an entire brain in miniature, – just as the faculty itself is really a specification of the entire man, a sort of homunculus.[36]

A literally identical statement holds for structure versus dynamism at the cellular and genetic levels.

So, here is where we stand. It is true that the present text is not about localizing symptoms, therefore explaining the link between neural dynamism and behavior by pointing to correlations and precise cortical coordinates seems futile. At the same time, to utterly disclaim the special stance of the cerebral cortex as a whole in the emergence of human traits would be incompatible with anatomical, physiological, neurological, developmental, and paleoanthropological databases. I suggest adopting what Flugel (1934) called "localization in the gross, but not in the fine"[37] and continue down this

[36] James (1950[1890], volume 1, p. 28–9).
[37] Flugel (1934, pp. 53–4).

path, aided by the conceptual nervous system, a framework that was presented and discussed in old-days behavioral psychology literature, adjusted to our needs.

The Conceptual Nervous System

Skinner coined the term *conceptual nervous system*, somewhat sarcastically, as a variation on the initials C.N.S. (Central Nervous System) in his 1938 book on *The Behavior of Organisms*.[38] Being critical about apparent over-simplification of neurophysiological concepts by psychologists in attempts to explain their behavioral findings, he states that "the essential advance from a description of behavior at its own level is, I submit, very slight. An explanation of behavior in conceptual terms of this sort would not be highly gratifying."[39] Twelve years later Skinner comes back to this term: "The writer's suggestion that the letters C.N.S. be regarded as representing, not the Central Nervous System, but the Conceptual Nervous System, seems to have been taken seriously";[40] there, in his analysis of psychological theories, he points to the (ab)use of the term, stressing that many psychologists who rely on neurophysiology to account for behavioral observations "are not talking about the nervous system as an actual structure undergoing physiological or bio-chemical changes but only as a system with a certain dynamic output."[41] Skinner explicitly calls for staying away from the influence of both kinds of C.N.S., central *as well as* conceptual, for they "create a false sense of security, an unwarranted satisfaction with the status quo," of not understanding relations between psychological variables.[42] While in a couple of pages what seems like a useful

[38] Skinner (1938).
[39] Ibid., pp. 421–2.
[40] In: "Are theories of learning necessary?," an address of the president, Mid-western Psychological Association, Chicago, Illinois, May, 1949; published in Skinner (1950, p. 194).
[41] Ibid.
[42] Ibid.

version of a conceptual nervous system is offered – useful, that is, in its applicability for the dialogue – Skinner's point on the false sense of security is of general importance and deserves much attention. Let us shortly derail the present stream of arguments and demonstrate Skinner's point on creating a false sense of understanding, for this tendency is definitely not unique to "neurologizing" psychologists. The reader is invited to contemplate Skinner's 1938 critical view while browsing through the following paragraph, extracted from a major textbook of neural science. A sample of words that are illuminating in that respect, are emphasized:

> Consider the act of hitting a tennis ball. For this task several sensory systems are **called** into play. Visual **information** about the motion of the approaching ball is **processed** in the visual system, which **identifies** the flying object and **computes** its direction and velocity. Proprioceptive information about the position of the player's arms, legs, and trunk in space are also **computed** by the brain to **plan** the appropriate positioning of the body for interception of the ball. All of this sensory information ultimately reaches multisensory **processing** regions in the cerebral cortex called association areas, where the **information is combined** to **elicit the memory** of earlier attempts to hit a tennis ball. In addition, the afferent information for the **planned behavior** recruits activity in the amygdala, a structure **concerned** with emotion and social behavior. The amygdala in turn activates the autonomic nervous system to **prepare** the body for action. Finally, brain systems **concerned** with voluntary movement are **recruited to initiate** the behavior. The multisensory association areas make connections with higher-order motor centers that **compute** a **program** for moving the racket into position. This **program is then passed** on to the primary motor cortex for **execution.**[43]

We do not know the meaning of "calling into play" in terms of neurons and synapses, nor the meaning of neural "processing" or "computation." We do not know what "plans" and "programs" are in

[43] Amaral (2000, pp. 317–18).

terms of synapses and neurons, and how (if at all) information theoretical concepts are relevant to the issues at hand, let alone how information is "combined" in a world of neurons and synapses, and how "programs" are "executed." The overall impression one obtains is that of a brain operating like a fancy restaurant, with efficient waiters running around, identifying new clients and their wishes, processing and translating to menu items, passing these over to the kitchen for preparation and execution according to preexisting recipes, feeding back to the waiters who pass on the output to the appropriate table. Of course, things sound more sophisticated when phrased in engineering and information theory terminology, but in their essence both terminologies subserve equally well "the false sense of security" that Skinner wants to avoid. Establishing a sense of security is attempted by concealing the absence of understanding by use of words from different languages. This is the epistemological minefield that brought Skinner to insist on adhering to the task of formulating the dynamic relations between behavioral observables.

A similar aura surrounds the sharp criticism of Boring (1929) on attempts to impose mathematical treatment as means to evade acknowledgment of misunderstanding: "a not uncommon case in science, in which inadequate data are treated with elaborate mathematics, the precision of which creates the illusion that the original data are as exact as the method of treatment."[44] With these words, written almost 90 years ago by a prominent historian of scientific psychology, it is difficult to avoid reflecting on the motivations of present-day large-scale initiatives to numerically simulate the brain, initiatives that (congruent with the extravagance of the twenty-first century) amount to much more than papers and pencils financed by the good will of tax-payers in Europe and America.

44 Boring (1929, p. 260), in the context of Johann F. Herbart's (1776–1841) mathematical treatment of simultaneously conscious "ideas."

Back to the term *conceptual nervous system*, which, after all, we do wish to make use of. It resurfaced in the title of Hebb's 1954 Presidential Address to the American Psychological Association: "Drives and the C.N.S. (Conceptual Nervous System)"[45] where he colorfully offers a practical approach, relying on advanced physiology that was not available in the earlier times that Skinner alludes to. Hebb writes:

> [T]he conceptual nervous system of 1930 was evidently like the gin that was being drunk about the same time; it was homemade and none too good, as Skinner pointed out, but it was also habit-forming; and the effort to escape has not really been successful. Prohibition is long past. If we *must* drink we can now get better liquor; likewise, the conceptual nervous system of 1930 is out of date and – if we *must* neurologize – let us use the best brand of neurology we can find. Though I personally favor both alcohol and neurologizing, in moderation, the point here does not assume that either is a good thing. The point is that psychology is intoxicating itself with a worse brand than it need use … Today's physiology suggests new psychological ideas, and I would like to persuade you that they make psychological sense, no matter how they originated.

Hebb's comment about "psychology intoxicating itself with a worse brand than it need" is relevant today as it was in 1954, especially regarding naive localization studies that are readily adopted by deferential followers from the discipline of psychology, whether these studies point to chemicals or receptors "associated" with attachment behavior, depression or schizophrenia, or brain structures involved in romantic love or engaged in a transference situation.

Let us adopt Hebb's spirit (no pun intended) and begin constructing a conceptual nervous system that is based on today's physiology. The resolution of the conceptual nervous system chosen here is dictated by only one thing: its potential to promote the dialogue between relational psychoanalytical and physiological frameworks. With this

[45] Published in Psychological Review, 1955.

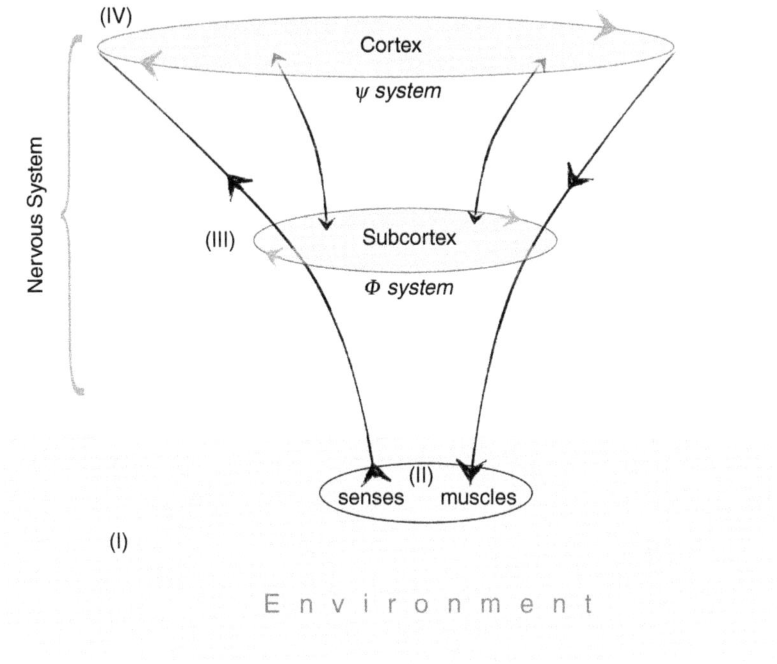

Figure 5.1. Conceptual Nervous System.

dictum in mind, a nervous system of the general form schematized in Figure 5.1 may be imagined, to be further developed and modified in later sections. The unbounded gray rectangle at the bottom, depicted (I), represents the open-ended, unfathomable environment, including all its generative relations as portrayed in Chapter 3. The nervous system is represented by two ovals, depicted (III) and (IV) that stand for *subcortex* and the *cortex*, respectively.[46] In Figure 5.1 the nervous system is separated from the environment, which is of course not the case; it is thus presented for clarity.

[46] A note for the anatomically educated reader: included in the conceptual cortex are both the isocortex (the six-layered neocortex) and the allocortex (the older, three-layered archicortex – hippocampus and olfactory cortex). Subcortical entities include the basal ganglia, diencephalon (thalamus, subthalamus, hypothalamus, and epithalamus), brainstem (midbrain, pons, and medulla), and the cerebellum.

The nervous system senses only a small sample of the relevant environment, including the states of our muscles; likewise, our muscles produce movements that impact on a very small sample of the relevant environmental processes and on our senses. These limited ranges of senses and movements are represented by the relatively small oval depicted (II). In our abstraction, sensing goes beyond the familiar five; it includes also receptors that are sensitive to concentrations of blood gases (oxygen, carbon dioxide), essential constituents (for instance, sugar, salts) and various hormones, as well as mechanical forces, volumes and tensions.

The different arrows of Figure 5.1 represent directions of propagated activities: from the senses to the subcortex and cortex, from the cortex and subcortical entities to the muscles, and self-reflecting loops, to and fro, between (black arrows) and within (gray arrows) subcortical entities and the cortex. Our body systems – muscles, heart, intestines, immune, endocrine, and so forth – are considered part of the environment, being outside the nervous system. Likewise, the sensing apparatuses are delegated to the *environment*. In short, everything that is not in the cortex or in the group of subcortical entities is considered environment from the point of view of the nervous system. This artificial cutoff between structures reflects their dynamism and will hopefully prove useful in the context of our analysis. A wider ellipse, wider compared to the subcortex, represents the cortex in Figure 5.1. The horizontal (width) dimension in the scheme stands for openness for change: the cortex has more capacity to be changed or reconfigured than the subcortex. This "openness for change" is reflected in the structure of the cortex, as will be explained. The general rule is that "climbing up" the anatomical ladder from the subcortex to the cortex entails increasing symmetry, loss of structure; as if the cortex is "less structurally committed" than the subcortex. This also means that the functionality of the cortex has to develop by experience rather than being dictated by predetermined programs and structures. Plasticity is by no means limited to the cortex, but the extent to which subcortical entities are capable of changing is a far cry from the cortex.

The form of two unfathomable spaces (environment and cortex) coupled through a narrow, structured, limited channel (sensory-motor envelope and subcortex) is not unrelated to model relations as presented in Chapter 3. Here, in the scheme of the conceptual nervous system, two spaces – rich internal and rich external worlds – communicate based on limited, scarcely sampled data. What does the external world "know" about the internal world, beyond that which is transmitted in movements? What can the internal space know about the outside world beyond that which is sparsely sampled by the senses? Viewed as such, the fact of even partially effective communication between subjects is remarkable.

The above exposition of the conceptual nervous system is rooted in physiological and psychological traditions. The bottom-up, subcortex to the cortex extension of symmetry and degrees of freedom, is designated in Figure 5.1 as Φ and Ψ systems; these are mnemonics to physiological (Φ) and psychological (Ψ) neural systems. They are added to the scheme of Figure 5.1 as a tribute to Freud's perceptive classification in his version of the conceptual nervous system, summarized in two notebooks, intensively written in September–October 1895 and immediately dispatched as attachments in a letter to Wilhelm Fliess (October 8). Freud's text became known as the *Project for a Scientific Psychology*.[47] In these notebooks Freud needed the separation between Φ-neurons and Ψ-neurons in order to account for the seemingly contradictory facts of stability and plasticity of the brain. Stability is meant in the sense of maintaining functional invariance; plasticity in the sense of being capable of adapting structure and function in reaction to changes in the environment or following tissue damage. The stability–plasticity conflict has challenged physiologists and psychologists over the past 150 years, from James and his

[47] Freud (1895, pp. 281–391).

contemporaries to present-day neurophysiologists.[48] In the more general engineering language of machine learning, the problem relates to the apparently conflicting demands that an adaptive apparatus must face, namely utilizing existing knowledge in order to maximize the reward while simultaneously changing the internal configuration of the machine (its very same knowledge) in search for enhanced performance: the exploration–exploitation tradeoff. Freud handled the problem by inventing memory networks, cells connected via "contact barriers" (synapses);[49] these contact barriers are capable of modifying their resistance to the transference of activity among "cathected neurons … filled with a certain quantity"[50] as a function of experience, thus constituting "vehicles of memory and, presumably of psychical processes in general."[51] These are to be contrasted with a stable class of cells that are connected via inert contact barriers, remaining relatively unchanged and thus supporting the "physiological" functions that need be stable. Freud named these two classes Ψ and Φ, respectively. A similar partition between the adaptive-memory (cortical, Ψ) system and the automated-"mechanistic" (subcortical, Φ) system, is described at length by James,[52] although the division there is less sharp; automated-mechanistic activity is also to be found in the cortical system, whereas adaptive-memory processes exist in lower, subcortical structures.

Following the footsteps of James, Freud, Hebb, and other prominent figures in the history of brain and behavioral science, many neurophysiologists and theorists find the general idea of a conceptual

48 N. Ziv phrases the problem along the tenacity–plasticity dimension; for example, Minerbi et al. (2009).

49 The term synapse was coined in 1897 by Sherrington, two years after Freud's Project for a scientific psychology was written.

50 Freud (1954, p. 358).

51 Ibid., p. 360.

52 James (1950[1890], vol. 1, ch. II).

nervous system useful, in spite of it being structurally dull compared to the actual nervous system. Indeed, the variance in the structures of neural systems within and between species, on the one hand, and the constancy of basic behavioral phenomena, across individuals and species, on the other, imply that the operation of the brain is governed by a set of underlying universal neural principles. These universals are realized in many different ways, in many different forms of neuroanatomy, hence justifying an abstract, conceptual approach.

Although the above conceptual approach to the nervous system is acknowledged, current major efforts of experimental neurobiology tend to emphasize specific realizations, such as particular forms of molecular machineries and specially arranged structures. These descriptions of specific realizations – both microscopic and macroscopic – are invaluable, especially for diagnostic and treatment-oriented purposes. This is true even when the action of underlying universals is unknown. But as far as comprehensive understanding is concerned, collecting facts about specific realizations is by itself insufficient and, at times, may be counterproductive. Given the complexity of neural systems, accumulation of such facts may lead the field astray rather than offer a coherent large picture. To understand how neural substrates may be related to behavior, one must understand the underlying universals common to all neural systems and their interaction with a dynamic environment. Thereafter, hypotheses regarding specific realizations and their constraints become tenable.

Neurophysiological Basics, a Digression

Consistent with the above, allocating space for detailed anatomical and cell-physiological facts about the brain is superfluous, as "too much anatomy has been found to order for theoretic purposes, even by the anatomists."[53] But, as young William James once wrote in a letter from the Amazonas (1865) while serving in a party led by Jean Agassiz: "No one sees farther into generalization than his own knowledge of details extends."[54] Therefor, several cell-physiological facts are highlighted below in the form of points that wrap together only the bare essentials for the dialogue. Readers who are familiar with the basic matters of cortical and subcortical dimensions, electrical phenomena in neurons, and synaptic communication, are encouraged to leaf through or skip this section.

Dimensions. The adult cortex is a convoluted plate that, unfolded, would occupy an area more-or-less equivalent to a 50x50 cm screen, 1.5–4.5 mm thick.[55] Having a well-defined anatomical division of the cortex to the right and left hemispheres, with complex relations between them, gave rise to fascinating and useful clinical neurology observations that are most relevant to issues of symptom localization, as discussed above. A considerable share of the clinical work in the field of neurology is dedicated to mapping behavioral symptoms to brain coordinates of suspected lesions such as hemorrhage, blood clot, tumor, or local infection; this is a first step in the formulation of diagnosis and application of physical, localized treatment. But we are already equipped with what is required in order to understand that neuroanatomical localization in general, and brain bi-laterality in particular, are of no immediate relevance to our intended dialogue. We simply take it as given – backed by ample experimental evidence – that psychological functions distribute within the total available neural space according to genetic, developmental, and adaptive constraints.

53 James (1950[1890], Volume 1, pp. 81–2).
54 *The Letters of William James*, 1920, vol. I, p. 65.
55 Readers interested in a more detailed account on cortical scales are encouraged to consult *Corticonics: Neural circuits of the cerebral cortex* (Abeles, 1991).

The cortex is densely packed with two types of cells: nerve (neurons) and glial cells. While glial cells are abundant, in fact outnumbering neurons,[56] the activity of neurons is unequivocally accepted as the major physiological correlate of behavior; we therefore neglect glial cells in our discussion.[57] The average number of neurons within one cubic millimeter of cortex is ca. 30,000 in the human (compared to 200,000 per cubic millimeter in the mouse). Estimates of the total number of neurons in the entire human cortex converge to ca. 20 billion; to intuit how large the number is, consider this: at the neuronal death rate of 50,000 per day – a realistic rate – it would take about 1,000 years to clear the cortex from neurons altogether. For all practical purposes the distribution of this huge number of neurons across the entire cortex is even. Thus, the reader is invited to picture the cortex, on the large scale, as a thick, homogeneous sheet, a symmetric structure that looks the same from wherever one chooses to observe it. An expert neuroanatomist would have to stretch his imagination in order to convince himself that he can tell one piece of cortex from another.

Subcortical entities are in general more structured, less symmetric. Note that the cortex holds ca. 18% of the entire population of neurons in the brain, packed within 70% of the brain's volume. It is in the cerebellum (the "little brain"), a structure that occupies about 10% of the brain's volume, situated at the lower-back region of our skulls, where the vast majority of the brain's neurons – ca. 80% – are situated. Cerebellar activity is mostly correlated with timing and

[56] See, for instance, a review article "How many neurons do you have? Some dogmas of quantitative neuroscience under revision" by Lent et al. (2012); see also "The human brain in numbers: a linearly scaled-up primate brain" by Herculano-Houzel (2009).

[57] Albeit intriguing reports on the involvement of glial cells in behaviorally relevant activities, their role in such processes remains marginal; glial cells' main function in the brain is supportive (biochemically and biophysically).

control of fine movements. All other subcortical entities[58] are populated by only ca. 2% of the total number of neurons in the brain. The fact that these 2% of neurons (buried deep within the skull) are packed in well-structured and anatomically resolved clusters (nuclei), has made them targets for intensive applied neurophysiological research and industry investment, a direct consequence of availability bias. The development of the cerebellum and these other subcortical nuclei do not show evolutionary changes that match the emergence of human traits. Following up on our discussion on localization, this last statement does not mean that subcortical entities are irrelevant to human-specific traits.

Salinity and its consequences – the origin of electrical phenomena in neurons. On the more microscopic scale one finds that, like practically all other tissues inside our body, the space between cells in the cortex is filled with a watery solution. This *extra-cellular* watery environment is salty, mainly due to the abundance of sodium and chloride ions, the dissolved components of table salt. The borders of a neuron, as every other cell in our body, are spatially defined by the *cell membrane*, a thin lipid covering that separates the interior of the neuron from its exterior. Having a markedly different composition of salts inside compared to the surrounding outside is the hallmark of a living cell. While the dominant ions composing the extra-cellular environment are sodium and chloride, the intracellular milieu is dominated by potassium ions and charged amino acids in proteins. There exist physiological reports claiming that as much as half the total neuronal energy expenditure is invested in maintenance of intracellular salt concentrations that differ from the extra-cellular ones.[59] A cell that loses its capacity to maintain an interior composition that differs from the exterior is dead, an association-provoking fact of the life sciences.

58 Basal ganglia, thalamus, sub-thalamus, hypo-thalamus, dorso-thalamus, midbrain, pons, and medulla.

59 Howarth, Gleeson, and Attwell (2012).

Ions are electrically charged atoms or molecules. The difference of ionic compositions between intra- and extra-cellular solutions leads to a major consequence, entailed by well-founded conservation relations: practically *all the cells in our body* maintain a negative electric potential inside, relative to the outside. It is safe to say that the average value of intracellular potential is roughly 0.06 volts negative compared to the extra-cellular potential.[60] This is called (in the physiological jargon) the *resting potential*. Most cells maintain a more-or-less stable negative resting potential that is used as an energy source for different biological activities. Neurons belong to a special class of cells that make use of this potential energy to generate electric signaling; the class is called *excitable cells*. Among the other members in the class of excitable cells one finds muscle cells, heart cells, hormone (for instance, insulin or adrenaline) secreting cells. Excitable cells are equipped with a machinery enabling them to transiently move away from the resting state, generating a positive, pulse-like, short change in membrane potential known as *action potential*. In cells of the heart and other body muscles, action potentials cause contraction in a beautifully organized process that translates electrical energy to movement; in hormone releasing (endocrine) cells the action potential brings about secretion of the hormone, which in turn spreads in body fluids and impacts the activity of target organs. In nerve cells, the action potential is a means to: (1) transmit external and internal sensory signals into the brain; (2) communicate among neurons within the brain; and (3) carry neuronal activity to muscles, hence generating movement, behavior.

The integrative nature of neurons – synapses (excitatory and inhibitory), dendrites, and axons. The structure of a single neuron,

60 Readers might wish to develop a sense for "how much is" 0.06 volts in terms of everyday life: considering the fact that this value of electric potential is focused across a thin cell membrane, the resulting electric field is close to the electric field that gives rise to bolts of lightning in a thunderstorm.

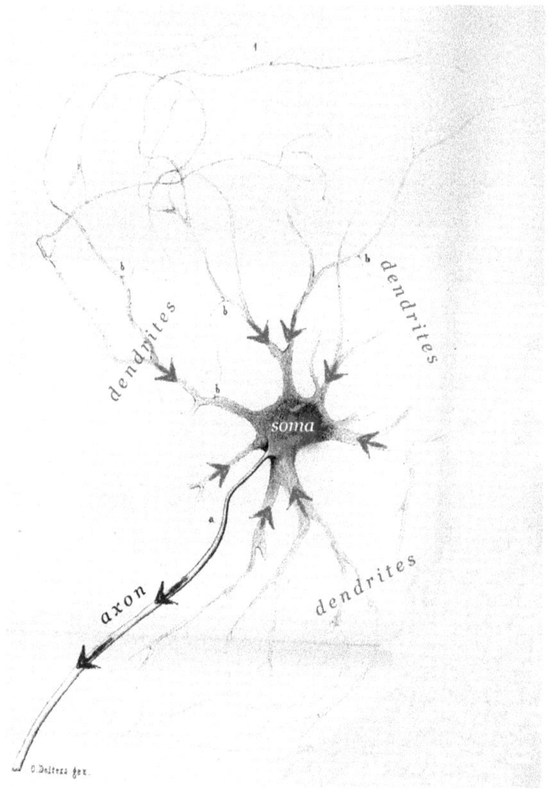

Figure 5.2. A nerve cell drawing by Otto Friedrich Karl Dieters (1834–1863); added arrows and text depicting dendrites and one axon.

when observed through a microscope, is complex. For our purposes it is useful to picture a generic form that has a set of receptive and effector branches (Figure 5.2). Receptive branches, called dendrites due to their tree-like shape, sense the activity of other ("upstream") neurons and propagate a modified form of this sensation to the cell body, the *soma*. If the integrated effect of the input to the soma crosses a *threshold* value (invariably more positive compared to the negative resting potential), an action potential is evoked in (and nearby) the soma. The mechanism of action potential generation in the soma of excitable cells is *the* canonical example of a well-understood phenomenon in the life sciences, mathematically, physically and biologically. This action potential, once evoked in the soma and its vicinity, is propagated through the effector branches that are called *axons* (a mnemonic for their axial shape), and impacts dendrites of many other, "downstream" neurons, which will be discussed shortly. The names *dendrite* and *axon* should not be taken too seriously as reflecting the actual shapes found under the microscope; the variability between different cortical neurons in this regard is immense.

The dendrites of each cortical neuron are decorated with many, probably thousands, of contact points with other neurons; these contact points are called *synapses*. Each synapse should be conceived as a sensor that detects the occurrence of an action potential in one given upstream (pre-synaptic) neuron somewhere in the cortex. When an action potential occurs in a given neuron, it travels down the axon of that neuron and releases packets of chemicals (neurotransmitters) in the synapses that the axon forms with other cells. The neurotransmitter molecules bind to the post-synaptic, dendritic side of the synapse, giving rise to a transient change in the local (near the synapse) intracellular potential. The transient effect of this *synaptic potential* relaxes back to the resting state after a fraction of a second.

The impact of the transient local synaptic potential depends on the identity of the pre-synaptic neuron, which may be one of the following: (1) an *excitatory neuron* – that is, a neuron that releases neurotransmitters that push its post-synaptic, downstream partners *toward the threshold*; or (2) an inhibitory neuron – that is, a neuron that releases neurotransmitters that push its post-synaptic, downstream partners *away from the threshold*. Excitatory and inhibitory neurons differ in the identity of the neurotransmitters that they synthesize and release. Thus, the direction of the effect in a given synaptic connection is fixed – that is, an inhibitory synapse remains inhibitory and an excitatory synapse remains excitatory; this is a property of the upstream neuron that is capable of synthesizing and releasing a uniquely defined neurotransmitter.[61] Many different kinds of neurotransmitters are known to act in the cortex, but for practical purposes we may classify them all as being either excitatory or inhibitory. There are thousands of synapses on the dendrites of any given cortical neuron; those that are activated by incoming excitatory neurons are accordingly denoted *excitatory synapses*; those that are activated by inhibitory incoming neurons are called *inhibitory synapses*. On top of its identity as excitatory or inhibitory, each synapse has one more identifier, that is – its "strength," the amplitude of the synaptic potential. Thus, the two identifiers of any given synapse are the direction of action (excitatory or inhibitory) and the strength of the change (strong or weak effects).

The transient synaptic potential (excitatory or inhibitory) propagates down the dendrite toward the cell body. It may safely be assumed that activation of one excitatory synapse is not enough to cause a cortical neuron to cross the threshold value and evoke an action potential. Estimates converge to several, maybe tens of excitatory synapses that need be active more-or-less simultaneously in order to drive the electrical potential in the soma above threshold. Thus a single synapse should be thought of as one point of entry into the cell, a point of entry that is either excitatory or inhibitory; one "vote" (for or against), counted by the downstream neuron. If the sum of votes amounts to above threshold, the neuron says "Aye" and emits an action potential. In that sense, a single neuron is said to be an integrator.[62]

Global neuromodulation. There is one more source of cortical neuronal activity modulation: chemicals that are "sprayed" onto the

[61] For completeness, note a counter example, a very special case that is irrelevant to our discussion reported in Wagner, Sagiv, and Yarom (2001), and references therein.

[62] This entire process is not deterministic; the critical role of "noisy" or "background noise" activity – that is, activity evoked by random variations in the dynamical constituents of the system, at practically each and every scale – is a subject matter for intensive research in physiology.

cortex, released from axons of subcortical neurons and change the cortical neuronal states globally. These chemicals are called neuromodulators and include dopamine, serotonin, norepinephrine, acetylcholine, and others. Their global effects on cortical neuronal activities do not lend themselves to any simple classification of the kind that serves us so well in the discussion of inhibitory and excitatory synapses. It is maybe useful to think of neuromodulators as nonspecific generators of variance, but let us defer discussion on this point to a more proper place in the text.

The Neuron Doctrine, Associationism, and the Network School

The neuron doctrine is a general term used to designate the understanding that brains are made of separate entities, neurons; the brain is not one spatially continuous compartment. The doctrine is a result of a collective effort that extended over 100 years, involving many scientists. It started with the development of advanced optical technology in the nineteenth century, which made it possible to observe specimens at high enough resolution. The technology was rapidly adopted by biologists; the leading physiologists in this context are people that we all know from cellular entities and cell-biology techniques called after their names: Jan Evangelista Purkinje (1787–1869), Theodor Schwann (1810–82), Camillo Golgi (1843–1926), Santiago Ramón y Cajal (1852–1934), and many others. Once the fact that brains are made of separate entities – neurons – was established, the natural question to ask was *how do neurons communicate with each other?* While the idea of chemical and electrical connectivity was out there for some time, it was Charles Scott Sherrington, just prior to 1900, who identified the gap within the contact points; Sherrington named the gap "synapsis." The first indication for communication across synapses by way of chemicals, again a widely accepted but abstract idea at the time, was made by Otto Loewi, the discoverer of acetylcholine, around 1920.[63] The neuron doctrine was fully wrapped and settled with the series of works beginning with Edgar Adrian and Yngve Zotterman (1926a,b): they were the first to demonstrate action potentials, the binary nature of action potentials, and their capacity to represent features of sensory stimuli by means of temporal firing patterns, as well as by changes in the rate of spiking.[64] Adrian and Zotterman's 1926 Journal of Physiology series of papers are a must-read for students of neurophysiology. It took another 25 years, and one more World War, before Alan Hodgkin and Andrew Huxley, Bernard Katz, John Eccles, and others deciphered the electro-chemical machinery underlying the generation of single fiber action potentials and their transformation to chemical transmission in the synapses.[65]

Thus, the journey to establish the neuron doctrine was completed 50–60 years ago, based on three tenets: morphology of the neuronal cell, the generation of spiking electrical activity, and the transmission of the activity between neurons via synapses. Many of the names mentioned above were awarded the Nobel Prize in physiology and medicine for their invaluable contributions.[66] Over the fifty years since the establishment of the neuron doctrine, a huge body of work was (and is) dedicated to what may brutally be summarized as characterization of the diversity of spatial and temporal scales involved in the three tenets of the neural doctrine: shapes of neuronal structures

[63] Interestingly, Loewi demonstrated the process in a cardiac preparation, something that is hard to imagine in our era, where many if not most neuroscientists that are educated in interdisciplinary schools are practically ignorant of general and system physiology, as if the brain is not an organ inseparable from the rest of physiology.

[64] The word "spike" is a physiologist's jargon synonymous to neuronal action potential. It is rarely used, if at all, to describe action potentials in excitable cells other than neurons.

[65] Most of the research reports from that physiological golden age are compiled in Cook and Lipkin (1972) Source Book.

[66] Camillo Golgi and Santiago Ramón y Cajal in 1906; Charles Sherrington and Edgar Adrian in 1932; Otto Loewi in 1936; John Eccles, Alan L. Hodgkin, and Andrew F. Huxley in 1963; Bernard Katz in 1970.

and their dynamics, forms of synaptic transmission and their dynamics, and forms of neuronal excitability and their dynamics.

The neuron doctrine reflects one of three interrelated strands of thought that constitute the most significant achievements of brain research over the past 150 years; we now turn to review briefly the development of the other strands, associationism and the neural network school. The sheer fact that simultaneous activation of several synapses is required in order to drive a cortical neuron beyond its threshold for action potential generation entails that behaviors – even the most simple ones imaginable – cannot be mapped to single action potentials generated by any one neuron. In a later part of this essay the term *neural activity group* is used in order to denote functional groups of action potentials that are emitted by populations of neurons in synchronic or diachronic manner. Neural activity groups are processes, formed and modulated throughout life in a dynamic, activity-dependent manner, conforming to evolution and environmental constraints. Neural activity groups are embedded in large populations of interconnected neurons, neural networks (Figure 5.3).

The concept of a neural network – albeit termed differently – has been used in psychology from its inception as an independent academic discipline. The foresight eminent psychologists had into the heart of modern concepts on neurons, synapses, and networks is impressive. Early references to this concept, dressed in a manner that directly corresponds with its present meanings, date back to Spencer's *The Principles of Psychology* (1855) and to Bain's *Mind and Body* (1874). Both attempted formulating behavior in terms of neurophysiological processes that involve communication lines between neurons, and modification of behavior (learning, adaptation) in terms of changes in "connexions efficacies." The idea underlying these early descriptions of neural networks is that experiencing co-incidence of events in the world shapes the individual's psychological realm. This idea of association by simultaneity dominates the psychological and neurophysiological discourse over, at least, 140 years. It is

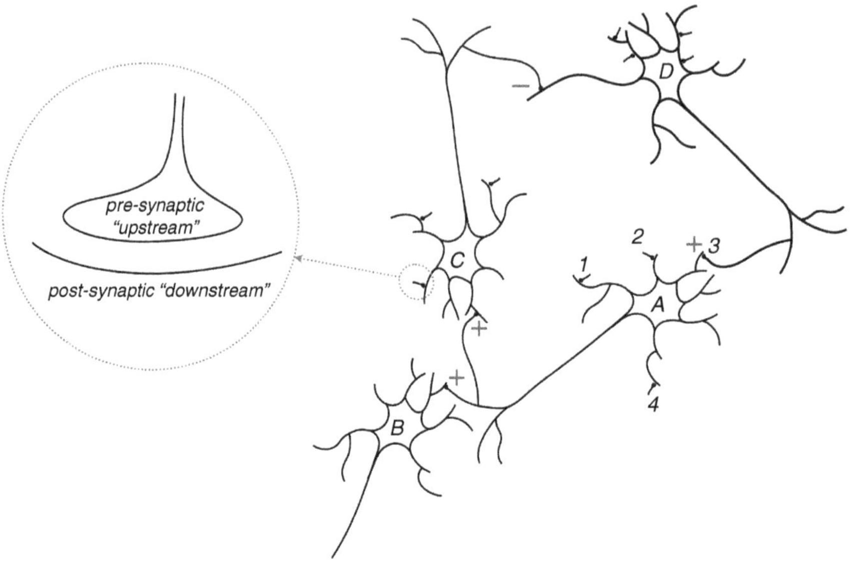

Figure 5.3. A caricature extract from a large network.
Explanation to Figure 5.3: Considering neuron A, only four (depicted 1 to 4) out of thousands of incoming synapses are depicted on its dendrites. Synapse number 3 is contributed by a branch of the axon of neuron D. Let us assume that neuron D is an excitatory neuron (depicted by positive sign in its outgoing synapses). Neuron A integrates the input from all of its synapses; if the integrated activity causes deviation from the resting potential beyond a threshold level, an action potential is evoked in neuron A. The action potential propagates down the axon of neuron A and activates the many synapses that this neuron contributes to other neurons. Let us assume that neuron A is an excitatory neuron. In the scheme of this figure, neuron A contributes synapses to neurons B and C. It also contributes synapses to hundreds or even thousands of other neurons, but we highlight only neurons B and C here. If the integrated activity of all the synapses on neuron C drives the neuron above threshold, then C generates an action potential. Let us assume that C is an inhibitory neuron. This means that the contribution of neuron C to the integration of neuron D is negative, inhibitory, pushing it away from the threshold potential, hence resisting its activation by other neurons. In the cortex, a neuron may contribute several synapses to another neuron. A scaled representation of a single synapse is shown to the left.

tightly related to the epistemological stance of empiricism in philosophy. Alexander Bain was probably the first to cast this psychological idea in modern terms,[67] as indicated in the following excerpt from his *Mind and Body* published in 1874, almost twenty-five years before Sherrington identified and defined the synapsis:

> I can suppose that, at first, each one of the circuits would affect all others indiscriminately; but that, in consequence of two of them being independently made active at the same moment (which is the fact in acquisition), a strengthened connexion or diminished obstruction would arise between these two, by a change wrought in the intervening cell-substance; and that, afterwards, the induction from one of these circuits would not be indiscriminate, but select; being comparatively strong towards one, and weaker towards the rest.[68]

It is – in the language used in this essay – a description of symmetry breaking *par excellence*. The idea of association by simultaneity is ubiquitous in James's writings, and clearly defined in his beautiful analysis of association (*The Principles of Psychology*, 1890): "When two elementary brain-processes have been active together or in an immediate succession, one of them, on reoccurring, tends to propagate its excitement into the other."[69] And it also appears in Freud, implicitly assumed as underlying his entire analytic framework, but explicitly defined within the neural network context in the *Project for a Scientific Psychology*: "There is, however, a fundamental law of

[67] Wilkes and Wade (1997); and references therein.

[68] Bain, *Mind and Body: the Theories of Their Relation* (1874, p. 119); the citation is extracted from an endnote that refers to insights derived from Lionel S. Beale's paper "Indications of the Paths Taken by the Nerve-Currents as They Traverse the Caudate Nerve-Cells of the Spinal Cord and Encephalon," published in the Proc. R. Soc. Lond. (1864). The text and the diagrams of neurons and their "connexions" in Beale's paper inspired several of Bain's ideas about the matter of the mind. Reading Beale's short paper is an aesthetic and teaching experience, even for the modern scholar.

[69] James (1950[1890], Volume 1, p. 566).

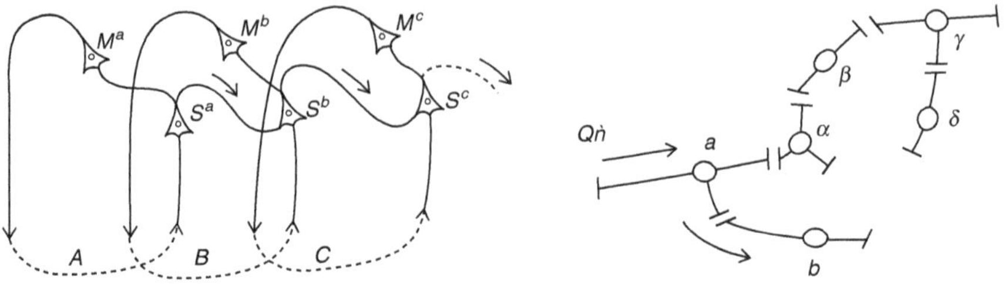

Figure 5.4. Both James and Freud used neural network schemes to explain the neurophysiological basis of behavior. Left: figure redrawn from James (1950[1890], volume 2, p. 588). Right: figure redrawn from Freud (1895, p. 324).

association by simultaneity, which operates during pure Ψ-activity... quantitative cathexis passes from one Ψ-neuron α to another β, if α and β have at some time been simultaneously cathected from Φ or elsewhere. Thus, the simultaneous cathexis α–β has led to the facilitation of a contact-barrier."[70] As already alluded to above, in Freud's terminology Φ (physiological) neurons are those whose synapses (contact barriers) are fixed, "retaining nothing";[71] Ψ (psychological) neurons are those that their synapses serve as vehicles for memory and "presumably, therefore, of psychical processes in general."[72] James and Freud thought in terms that are identical to associationism and the school of neural networks that dominates the present day. The two schemes of Figure 5.4 speak for themselves.

And, finally, Hebb in *The Organization of Behavior* (1949) literally re-cites Freud and proposes: "When an axon of cell A is near enough to excite a cell B and repeatedly or persistently takes part in firing it, some growth process or metabolic change takes place in one or both cells such that A's efficiency, as one of the cells firing B, is increased."[73]

[70] *The origins of Psycho-Analysis: Letters to Wilhelm Fliess, Drafts and Notes: 1887–1902*, p. 380.
[71] Ibid., p. 360.
[72] Ibid.
[73] Hebb (1949, p. 62).

Nowadays, neurophysiologists name this principle of association by simultaneity *Hebb's Rule*, and as can be imagined it encompasses a family of association principles that differ from each other in their dependence on the temporal structure of activities in the neurons flanking the synapse. Guided by considerations of physical conservation, modern physiologists have expanded the principle of association by simultaneity, proposed and identified a complementary set of rules that take care of synaptic *disassociation.* This entire topic goes under the term "spike timing dependent plasticity."

We have already mentioned that the word synapsis or, as now known synapse, was coined by Sherrington in 1897, two years *after* Freud's letter to Fliess,[74] a fact that makes the experience of leafing through Freud's *Project* no less than astonishing. Freud used the term contact barrier to describe the junction between neurons. In Freud's terminology, contact barriers may be "facilitated," having their "resistances" reduced following the law of association by simultaneity. Thus Freud marks, many years before Hebb, the link between synaptic plasticity and memory:

> Here is the argument ... their contact-barriers are brought into permanently altered condition. And since psychological experience tells us that there is such a thing as progressive learning based on recollection, this alteration must consist in the contact-barriers becoming more capable of conduction – less impermeable ... We shall describe this condition of the contact-barriers as their degree of 'facilitation' ['Bahnung']. We can then assert that *memory is represented by the facilitations existing between Ψ-neurons.*[75]

Probably noted by others, it is interesting to discover, in reading the *Project*, words that were coined by Freud to depict processes at

[74] Bennett (1999).

[75] This particular citation is the translation of Freud's 1895 *Project* as it appears in Freud (1954, p. 361); italics in the original. The same text is translated slightly different in the standard edition (Freud, 1895, p. 300), but conveys the same meaning.

the neural network level, later acquiring rich psychoanalytical meanings: for example, *resistance* (of "contact barriers") to *transference* of neuronal *cathexis* (his term for a phenomenon nowadays known as "action potential" or nerve "spike").

We end this historical perspective on the neuron doctrine, associationism, and the network school with a perceptive comment made by Flugel (1934) on the roots of the correspondence between memories or ideas and synapses. Flugel describes how, in 1833, taking advantage of recent improvements to the microscope, Robert Remak discovered that the brain is built of cells rather than being an amorphous medium, a landmark finding that in later years – following the works of Golgi, Cajal, and many others – led to the formulation of the neuron doctrine.[76] Flugel asks what made the finding of brain being composed of cells so appealing and influential, from those early days to the time of his analysis (1934) and, in fact, to present days. Flugel's answer is so deep and relevant to the subject matter of the present essay, that I cannot resist bringing it here almost in full. Flugel points to an apparent

> parallelism between the structure of the brain that histological research was just revealing and the nature of the mind as pictured by the associationism which was the dominant psychological doctrine of the period and which had just found such a consistent and thoroughgoing exponent in James Mill. Associationism regarded the mind as composed of a great number of elementary units, the 'ideas', linked together into combinations of varying degrees of closeness and complexity and continually forming new connections with one another; the phenomena of mind, as revealed by introspection, consisted indeed, it was supposed, in this very process of connection. Histology was now showing that the nervous system, on its side, was composed of innumerable simple units, the cells, linked

[76] The story of Robert Remak's underestimated scientific contributions, titled: "A Polish, Jewish Scientist in 19th-Century Prussia" is summarized in a one-page historical note by David Lagunoff, published in Science, 2002.

> together by a tangle of connecting fibres, admirably suited, it would seem, to serve as the physical substrate of the 'associations' observed in consciousness. What more natural than to suppose that the individual cells somehow corresponded to elementary ideas and the nerve fibres connecting the cells to their associations? That complex ideas corresponded to a group of interconnected cells, and so on? The appearance of an idea in consciousness would then correspond to the occurrence of some process in the corresponding cell or cells, while an association of ideas would imply the passage of an impulse along the fibres linking the cells in question. It is true that further reflection showed that there were difficulties in the way of such a very simple and obvious scheme of correspondence. On the psychological side, for instance, it was difficult to determine the precise nature of the really irreducible and elementary idea that would correspond to a single nerve cell. On the physiological side, cells were not confined to the nervous tissue, but were found throughout the bodies of animals and plants. Within the nervous system they were found not only in the brain but in the spinal cord and in various isolated ganglia, which did not appear to have direct relation to consciousness ... This view of the correspondence really presupposed a cerebral localization far more extreme even than that of phrenology, which only sought to localize some thirty-seven faculties, not countless numbers of ideas.[77]

Flugel's reflections on the simplistic correspondence between a network of ideas and a network of neurons, in other words between philosophically based associationism and biologically based neuron doctrine, are insightful. These reflections are as relevant today as they were in 1934. To his comment on the difficulty entailed by lack of an elementary psychological "particle" we have referred in our discussion on the irreducibility of psychological concepts. The second difficulty raised by Flugel relates to the physiological side: cellular networks with various connectivities and complexities are ubiquitous in physiology and biology; what makes neural networks unique in that they (but not other networks) form the mind?

[77] Flugel (1934, pp. 55–6).

One approach to this question involves a search for special neurons or groups of neurons or special networks, the structure of which is uniquely suited to bring about the conscious mind. We have already discussed this naive reductionism in earlier pages of this essay. The other direction, more to my taste, has to do with the definition of cognitive sciences at large, where neural networks are not treated as unique elements that cater to a psychological mind; rather *networks of neurons are but one of many possible instantiations of a type that may be used in the realization of a system that behaves.* This is not to deny the importance of the neuronal instantiation, which is intimately related to us in the general and the practical aspects as humans. But it is a most inspiring challenge for science to define what are the constraints involved in making networks of *abstract* coupled elements cognitive, self-reflecting, "psychological" subjects.

We now turn to describe processes and entities in a conceptual nervous system, processes and entities that might correspond to the primitives of relational objects in psychology: *inner space, discontent, symmetry breaking,* and the *emergence of objects, inter-object interactions,* and *adaptation.*

Symmetry and Self-Reflexive Inner Physiological Space

We have seen in Chapter 4 that the *psychological inner space*, mostly distant from awareness, is often referred to as ego, the seat of phantasies. This inner space is a reflexive entity, characterized by the self-engaging dynamism of interpretation and projection among its internal constituents, a dynamism that is sensitive – within limits – to external events. At birth this inner space is occupied by primitive phantasies (proxies for physiological infantile reflexes) that, when triggered by environmental cues (stimuli), satisfy basic instincts. The concept of the primal symmetry of the inner space was offered in reference to a utopian situation where all the instinctual needs are provided by means of the environment (mother) and the primitive phantasies.

In a short text titled "The Common Sensorium: An Essay on the Cerebral Cortex,"[78] Valentino Braitenberg offers a masterful integration of cortex anatomy and physiology, "abstracting away from the local (i.e., within one brain) and interspecific variations."[79] The content of the following pages is based on Braitenberg's exposition, interpreted and furnished with numbers, facts, and ideas that seem relevant to our purpose – that is, describing the physiological inner space with the psychological theory of relational objects in mind.

In reference to the type of symmetry that dominates the cortical neural network, Braitenberg points to the fact that the cortex is, by and large, uniform, with horizontal connections that may extend to the scale of the whole organ, evenly distributed in all directions. This is in contrast to the vertical axis, where symmetry is broken. What we are asked to imagine is akin to a stack of neuronal layers, like a layered cake. While each layer looks more-or-less the same throughout the cortex, the layers qualitatively differ from each other in the shapes of neurons they accommodate, and the connectivity among these neurons (within a layer), as well as in the patterns of connections between each layer and all other layers. Thus, *along the horizontal axes the cortex is symmetric* (that is, it makes no difference where one cuts it), but *the vertical axis is highly structured, asymmetric*. Going top-down gives a different order of things compared to going bottom-up. The anatomical symmetry of the horizontal plane has consequences:

> The absence of well-defined boundaries within the gray substance, the fact that every small region of gray substance contains pieces of dendrites and axons belonging to neurons of the same gray substance,

[78] Braitenberg (1977[1973]), chapter 8 of his book *On the Texture of Brains: An Introduction to Neuroanatomy for the Cybernetically Minded.*

[79] Ibid., p. 101.

> situated at distances that may be very large compared to the macroscopic dimensions of the whole organ, suggests that such an organ functions as a whole … [This] is in contrast to the popular view of the cortex as composed of sensory, motor and associational regions.[80]

In fact, this picture is in contrast to the spirit of localization as an explanation to the operation of the brain, in the large as well as in the small scales. This is already familiar to us from the discussion on localization. The explanatory status of localization in relation to the workings of the brain resembles the explanatory status of a keyboard layout in relation to the mechanism underlying word processing software: a non-unique arrangement, determined by the particulars of the historical evolution, and – to a large extent – adaptive. The point of analogy to localization is the irrelevance of the particular layout to the understanding of the typewriter mechanism, let alone the software and hardware underlying computerized word processing.[81]

The *asymmetric* layered columnar structure that looks the same throughout the cortex, taken together with the horizontal plane *symmetry* "corresponds to the fundamental operation that the cerebral cortex performs on its input. This should be an operation between layers, with one or more layers of the cortex serving as input stations and the other layers as output."[82] Quite a lot is known about the propagation of activity across the different layers on the small scale – that is, along the asymmetric vertical axis that is the carrier of the

80 Ibid., pp. 102–4.

81 A combinatorial large number of other layouts would do, but C. Latham Sholes (1819–90) is said to have designed the common QWERTY layout based on the frequency of letter pairs in American English, to prevent jamming of nearby key-bars in the mechanical typewriter produced and distributed by *Remington & Sons* (manufacturers of guns and typewriters). Over the years, keyboard layouts were adapted to different languages, new symbols, and so forth, but QWERTY remained dominant, even though the phenomenon of type-bars clashing and jamming is absolutely meaningless in computer keyboards.

82 Braitenberg (1977[1973], p. 105).

fundamental operation. For our purposes it is enough to summarize this knowledge as follows: Axons that conduct electrical activity from outside the cortex synapse onto neurons in the lower cortical layers.[83] Within the cortex, the activity propagates up the axons of the lower layer neurons, activating neurons of upper layers. These, in turn, synapse *locally* and activate nearby neurons. The local activity propagates *down and out* the cortex via output axons. The popular distinction of "white" and "gray" matter relates to the axons (incoming and outgoing) and the layers, respectively.[84]

The gray matter of the cortex (the layers) is not a passive entity; it is continuously active also in the absence of signals from the incoming axons. This is seen in measurements under conditions where all incoming axons are disconnected.[85] In fact, even when networks of cortical neurons are cultivated outside the brain, spontaneous activity is a pronounced, ubiquitous default feature that is difficult to avoid even under well-controlled conditions.[86] Thus, our physiological inner space is dominated by intrinsic, ongoing activity in the absence of external input, an observation that is highly relevant to the dialogue. Moreover, an extensive set of observations indicates that at the very early stages of development, the intrinsic ongoing activity of cortical networks has a global, synchronized, all-encompassing nature; if one neuron is active at a given point in time, it is highly likely that most other neurons in the cortex are active, more-or-less synchronously.[87] This symmetry is broken by functional interaction

83 For a recent analysis see "Deep Cortical Layers Are Activated Directly by Thalamus" by Constantinople and Bruno (2013); and references therein.

84 Incoming and outgoing axons are histologically different from local (intra-cortex) axons; under the microscope, the latter look gray whereas the former white. The white color of axons that enter or leave the cortex is due to a cellular coating of these axons that caters to faster propagation, which is critical when long distance connections are concerned.

85 For example, Timofeev et al. (2000).

86 Reviewed in Marom and Shahaf (2002).

87 Ibid.

with the world as the brain matures, a developmental process we will relate to in subsequent sections.

Related to this intrinsic dynamism, Braitenberg directs our attention to one more telling neuroanatomical fact, which concerns the origins and targets of the white matter (incoming and outgoing axons). Most of the neurons in the gray matter send axons down and out of the cortex. The majority of these white matter axons (amounting to ca. 10^{10}) travels a distance beneath the gray matter and reenter the cortex in different places. All other sources of incoming axons amount to less than 10^7 (that is, less than 0.1% of the total incoming axons). Braitenberg concludes that

> [M]ost of the work the cortex does is on information that it itself provides. It seems that the cortex acts mainly and essentially in a *reflexive mode*. We are not surprised about this since it is intuitively obvious (and confirmed by many observations of experimental psychology) that our perceptions are always a mixture of a little input from the sensory channels with abundant information already present in memory.[88]

Cortical reflexive dynamism may also be inferred by considering other quantitative aspects of primate neuroanatomy. Careful measurements show that the white matter (consisting of connections *between* cortical areas) occupies a volume that is nearly equal to that of the gray matter (the layers) in man.[89] Comparative analyses indicate that the volume of cortical white matter increases disproportionally with gray matter volume.[90] Specifically, white matter volume, across many species of mammals,[91] more-or-less equals gray matter volume raised to the power of 4/3, leading to white matter "runaway." For instance, of the total cortex volume in the shrew, which is just above 10 mm^3,

88 Braitenberg (1977[1973], p. 106).
89 Miller, Alston, and Corsellis (1980).
90 Bush and Allman (2003); and references therein.
91 Zhang and Sejnowski (2000).

white matter occupies less than 10%; in man, where the total cortex volume is around 1,000 mm^3, the white matter occupies almost 50%. Braitenberg presented a convincing back of the envelope calculation, already in 1973, showing that the rough assumption of every point connected to every other point in the cortex is compatible with the above gross anatomy data.[92] Taken together with the elegant analytical treatment by Zhang and Sejnowski,[93] it becomes clear that the disproportionate increase of white matter compared to gray matter arises as a natural consequence of cortex symmetry and the compactness of its connections.

Moreover, the folded nature of the cortex, maybe the most immediate image that each of us has in mind when thinking about the brain, is tightly related to the compactness of connectivity. Cortical folding increases the ratio of actual to exposed surface contours by a factor of about three.[94] The old view, that the cortex is so extensively folded simply because there is not enough room for so many neurons within the cranial cavity, turns out to be much too simplistic. It is now believed that these folds (known as *gyri*) reduce the cost that brains pay – in terms of white matter volume – on enlarged cortical surface area; this is achieved by tension-based shortening of distances between remote regions that are highly connected.[95] Braitenberg summarizes these anatomical and physiological facts about the cortex: *"Altogether we arrive at the picture of the cortex as a gigantic mixing machine. Every small bit of the cortical gray substance contains information about the state of a very large number of cortical cells."*[96]

We have focused our attention on the cortex but, as depicted in the conceptual nervous system of Figure 5.1, reflexive dynamism that

92 Braitenberg (1977[1973], p. 114).
93 Zhang and Sejnowski (2000).
94 Zilles et al. (1988).
95 Van Essen (1997). For a comprehensive review on the economy of brain network organization, see Bullmore and Sporns (2012).
96 Braitenberg (1977[1973], p. 114).

is based on anatomical symmetry is not unique to the cortex. It is the hallmark of the nervous system as a whole. If one is to name but one feature of the brain, it is symmetry-based self-reflexion.

In the description of psychological inner space we referred to the symmetry as "primal," a substrate for the effects of serial psychological symmetry breaking events throughout development. Later in this chapter a section is dedicated to means of physiological symmetry breaking and the emergence of physiological objects. But it is tempting to put forward an argument, already at this point, to convince ourselves that congruence between physiological and psychological inner spaces is to be expected. It is an argument from infant neurological development. The hierarchical nature of the conceptual nervous system is reflected in the normal and the pathological spectrum of neurological phenomena. The breaking up from primitive reflexes during the first few months of development is a teaching example to that matter. Earlier, infantile reflexes are equated with the Kleinian notion of primitive phantasies, inborn hypotheses about the world, constituting what Segal called "crude phantasy life" that exists from birth.[97] Grasp, Moro, rooting, stepping and other infantile reflexes make sense from the phylogenetic perspective as "first guesses" for movements that promote survival. Some of these reflexes remain intact in the anencephalic newborns, tragic cases where the newborn comes to the world without a cortex,[98] indicating, as now accepted among neonatologists, that these reflexes are generated by subcortical entities. The disappearance of infantile reflexes with development is due to their inhibition by cortical circuits that evolve over the first several months of living.[99] In other words, the inappropriateness of exercising primitive reflexes in different (relational, in the broad sense) contexts is something that is learned, probably by constructing

97 Segal (1975, pp. 13–23).
98 Reviewed in Futagi, Toribe, and Suzuki (2012).
99 Ibid.; and references therein.

what Bowlby imagined as "working models of the world and of himself [the child] in it."[100] Congruent with this conclusion, damage to the cortex might cause their reappearance in the adult. The general principle seems to be a symmetric (that is, context-insensitive) set of primitive phantasies that the newborn comes to the world with, a symmetry that is broken by selective cortical inhibition in relation to real world interactions.

This principle of symmetry breaking by inhibition resurfaces in many psychological and neurophysiological contexts, as well as in the larger biological context. It was already recognized in the late nineteenth century, following Hughlings Jackson's[101] ideas on "levels" of brain organization, where higher levels impose patterns on lower ones by means of inhibition. Flugel (1934)[102] comments on the concept of pattern formation (symmetry breaking) by inhibition, a concept that gradually gained importance in brain and behavioral research

> ... [once] realized, through the work of Sherrington and others, that higher centers, and especially the cortex, normally exercise an inhibiting effect upon the function of the lower centers. This is apparently a discovery of very great significance, since if there is failure on the part of the higher centers, or the nervous paths through which their control is exercised, the lower centers, released from this control, begin to function with unusual vigor and freedom. This 'over-reaction' may be useful for determining the existence of higher level defect, and also for ascertaining the functions of the lower centers, which are revealed more clearly in their exaggerated form. *Quite generally, the concept of control or* [by?] *inhibition was coming to be of increasing importance both in neurology and psychology, ... soon to become one of the most essential elements in the whole modern picture of the mind.* [italics added]

100 Bowlby (1973, p. 203).
101 A British neurologist (1835–1911), most known for his seminal contributions to epileptology.
102 Flugel (1934, pp. 223–4).

Several features of the psychological inner space are discussed, interpreted to physiology and projected back: primal symmetry, the reflexive nature of self-engaging dynamism, as well as the sensitivity – within limits – to external events. Moreover, the developmental timeline of infantile reflexes is encouraging in the sense that these key features have the potential to support other primitives of the psychological objects relations. Yet, this passage has neglected a major aspect of the psychological inner space: its being, mostly, distant from awareness. What can we, physiologists, do with this psychological concept? What can we say about awareness without sinking into the age old philosophical debates that concern consciousness?[103] Does awareness lend itself to a meaningful dialogue between psychological and physiological object relations? Is it at all possible to have a meaningful dialogue between depth psychology and physiology without stepping over such philosophical mines? It is not clear what the answers to these questions are; all one may offer is one's own biased view on these matters, acknowledging that there is room for other, very different approaches. Despite heroic endeavors to identify various neural correlates of the phenomenon, I tend to believe that awareness – and more generally consciousness – is a psychological concept that cannot be mapped to physiology in the language relation sense of Chapter 3 without loss of meaning. Hence we limited ourselves from the outset by defining behavior as that which is expressed in movements, a definition that should help us keep distance from such murky zones. What about activity *that does not leave* the cortex (or subcortex) toward the muscles – that is, brain activity that is not expressed in some form of somatic mechanics (movements or secretions)? I do not know the answer to this question, although it is difficult for me to imagine consciousness in general, and awareness in particular, as independent of ongoing, streamed

[103] The terms awareness and consciousness are left undefined; awareness is assumed to be one key expression of consciousness.

relations of movements and sensations, pragmatic in their Jamesian meaning of coupled or relational dynamics. Viewing consciousness in general, and awareness in particular, as independent of ongoing movement–sensation negotiations with the environment,[104] amounts to attributing consciousness or mindfulness to a cluster of biological cells connected to each other in one way or another, situated in the skull or on top of a laboratory bench, or in a test tube. We have already mentioned the epistemological quicksand to which this kind of naive reductionism submits itself. In the context of the present essay, the farthest the dialogue on the subject – that is, psychological inner space being largely distant from awareness – is taken, is to point at an intriguing physiological parallel: the vast majority of brain electrical activity is not immediately or directly available to the muscles. Likewise, the major part of electrical activity generated by the sensing organs is not directly or immediately available to a significant portion of the gray matter.[105]

From the point of view of a physiologist seeking introduction of meaning to basic physiological and anatomical facts through dialogue with depth psychology, the symmetric nature of the conceptual nervous system, its entailed reflexive dynamism and its remoteness from the sensory-motor envelope are encouraging. We now turn to examine machineries that avail breaking the primal physio-anatomical symmetry.

104 Environment as defined in the conceptual nervous system is everything that is outside the brain, including the subject's body.

105 Not unrelated, the fact that the brain itself is physically insensitive to the same types of peripheral stimuli that activate it is fascinating. This is apparent in awake craniotomy, a common medical procedure where patients go through a brain operation while remaining awake. In these procedures, the brain is touched, cut, heated, and electrified, while the patient feels no pain. The patient does move his muscles and reports various feelings and impressions, but no pain is felt. In other words, the very organ that interprets all sensory stimuli has no sensory envelope to report on its own physical interactions with the world, but through movements (muscles) or secretions (glands).

Symmetry Breaking, Programs, and Dynamics

Symmetry, reflexive dynamism, and remoteness from the sensory-motor envelope (the layer that is actually in contact with the outer world), entail a challenge to an evolving adaptive system. This is due to the fact that activity – in whichever point one chooses to observe within the conceptual nervous system – is not a unique, faithful representative of sensory features. Rather, neural activity is the outcome of sensory input, convolved with self-sustained internal dynamism and the remains of past sensory impacts. While situated *in utero*, the challenge of evolved adaptivity is substantially diminished. This is due to the fact of the fetus being fed by the placenta, an "inert" physiological organ that negotiates with the mother's blood, no matter what pattern of spontaneous (or stimulus evoked) activity takes place in the nervous system, and regardless of the resulting movements. Fairbairn, as discussed in Chapter 4, relates to this utopian setting as the "theoretically perfect conditions," where frustration (discontent) – the engine of symmetry breaking and consequent mental development – "could hardly arise."[106] But for the infant in the outer world, where basic needs depend on a subjective caregiver, the scenario is completely different. Outside the uterus, the relational context makes stimulus ambiguity inevitable, and the infant's movements in these relations with the mother subject do matter. The external object – be it the mother or her breast – appears more-or-less the same in the contrastive, nourishing–retreating situations. The same external object calls for different evoked patterns of brain activity that translate to movements (to suck or to bite?). The challenge faced by the infant is significant even if we do what should not be done – to ignore the relational context. From the physical point of view, the external object in these two situations is *almost* identical, or better said – identical at the large: under both conditions a similar set of

[106] Fairbairn (1944).

sensory receptors is activated because the physical stimulus features involved are similar (same physical mother, same physical breast). But there are differences; there must be, in the small, in the fine details – tension, softness, a gesture here or a tone of voice there – between the nourishing good and the retreating bad external objects. The mental task of the developing infant is to figure out the situation, to classify (based on these fine details) the two presentations of the external object.

The ambiguous situation may be thought of in physiological terms as activation of the conceptual nervous system in two "nearby" points. The physiological task of the developing nervous system of the infant is to be able to classify these nearby inputs, giving rise to adaptive and properly matched activities that are reflected in advantageous movements. To some (crude) extent this is given, built into the infantile reflexes. But relying on these predefined reflex patterns is not good enough for higher order organisms; we live in a relational reality that is much too ambiguous for these early phantasies or preliminary hypotheses to suffice. The resolution of the ambiguity is achieved by symmetry breaking and formation of preferred propagation paths within the gray matter.

Given the primal symmetry and ongoing reflexive dynamism that is imposed by the restraining vote of a large population, billions of coupled neurons, the task of adapting the patterns of brain activity to these early and unforeseen relational finesses is formidable. The resolution of the ambiguity is no less than fate determining. This is a neurodevelopmental parallel of the more universal process that biologists describe in the early stages of embryogenesis, progression from a symmetric "omnipotent" structure, to one singled-out realization.

The metaphor I have in mind when contemplating the rupture in the infant's brain – as well as in his or her psyche for that matter – is *gastrulation*, a generic developmental process where an embryonic symmetric sphere of cells folds in, thus creating multiple layers of cells that are arranged along a head–tail axis from which body organs

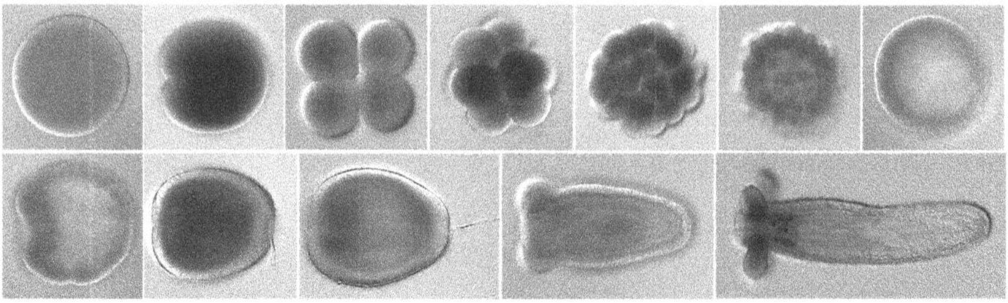

Figure 5.5. Embryonic development in *Nematostella vectensis*, a sea anemone. Various stages of hierarchical symmetry breaking over seven days, starting from an egg (top-left; diameter ca. 250 μm), progressing with a series of cleavages to a blastula (top-right, a hollow sphere surrounded by cells), through gastrulation (bottom-left), to a feeding juvenile polyp (bottom-right; length ca. 800 μm).
Image reproduced from Lee et al. (2007), with permission.

emerge. It is the most dramatic symmetry breaking process in the development of an organism (demonstrated in Figure 5.5). Lewis Wolpert, a renowned developmental biologist, is credited with the celebrated observation: "It is not birth, marriage, or death, but gastrulation which is truly the most important time in your life." The resemblance, in spirit and image, to Freud's words on the ". . . . rift in the ego which never heals but which increases as time goes on,"[107] cannot be missed. How should we approach the physiological interpretation of psychological symmetry breaking? What is the kind of explanation provided by science to such sequences of seemingly well-structured and literally future forging events?

Whether interpreting evolutionary or developmental processes, embryogenesis or neural or mental adaptations, we find ourselves positioned somewhere along a spectrum that extends between two polar stances, a position that reflects personal biases and capacities, history of education, and availability of experimental and analytic tools. One pole may be called the *structural–programmatic* stance,

[107] Freud (1938).

which is immediately suggested by observing processes like the embryogenesis of Figure 5.5. This is the stance from where development seems to progress in a precisely timed manner through a predetermined program. It is indeed difficult to resist interpreting the series of snapshots shown in Figure 5.5 as following a program leading from one stage to the next. The structural–programmatic stance entails a search for the programmed sequence of events and the identity and location of the elements that carry out (or are in-charge of) each event, the coordinates of these elements, and the fields and forces they exert on each other. This stance calls for explaining what went wrong in the algorithm when the resulting pattern deviates from the expected – that is, when the program and its elementary particles fail to deliver. Scientists who adhere to this stance often rank the presumed programs in terms of their optimality vis-à-vis the aimed for results, drifting toward measures and methods that are applied in advanced domains of engineering and information theory. Naturally, the structural-programmatic stance is tightly related to the applied aspects of life sciences and, as such, stresses individual differences in the structure.

As discussed in the last chapter of this book, the structural–programmatic stance is rooted in human culture. In its extreme version it reflects a need to believe that things have well-defined causes that are situated in well-defined coordinates. But such extreme expressions of the structural–programmatic stance are challenged by the extent to which developmental processes are plastic. For instance, embryogenesis adapts itself to various unforeseen manipulations, including the removal or addition of cells;[108] likewise, cortical organization is impressively plastic, changing dramatically to accommodate unforeseen lesions.[109] Such observations

108 Reviewed in, for example, Wennekamp et al. (2013).

109 Reviewed in, for example, Buonomano and Merzenich (1998) and Xerri (2012).

are incompatible with a programmatic stance, strictly defined. More generally, the very fact of phylogeny and ontogeny that are adaptive to unforeseen challenges is incompatible with the concept of a program, strictly defined. This criticism cannot be relaxed by addition of conditionals (If–Then expressions) to the program; for an If–Then, the If should be a priori defined, poling apart from the very meaning of the term 'unforeseen'.

The above constraints are usually taken as reasons for coming up with the alternative, *functional–dynamic* stance. In its extreme expression, the functional–dynamic stance attributes the wisdom of living to the whole complex, which includes the developing system *together with* the ambience, the environment within which the developing system is situated; it is the environment that molds the structures and patterns of the developing system, by way of meaningful interactions. This stance entails focusing on generalities, formulations in terms of self-organization, coupled dynamical systems, identifications of constraints and limits, mean-fields, and distributions rather than individual cases. Chances that a functional–dynamic point of view gives rise to useful, applied implementations are low when compared to those of the structural–programmatic approach.

Both stances, the structural–programmatic and the functional–dynamic, come in many different flavors and, accordingly, have many different names in philosophy, Edelman's "isms."[110] Interesting as it is, given my limited perspective of philosophical intricacies it is probably better to avoid a discussion that relates these various "isms" to the overtly simplistic structural–programmatic functional–dynamic dimension described above. Having said this, it is acknowledged that the tension between structural–programmatic

[110] G.M. Edelman, *Bright Air, Brilliant Fire: On the Matter of the Mind*, 1992, p. 158 ("A Graveyard of Isms: Philosophy and Its Claims"); Edelman's bold position concerning philosophy in general, and epistemology in particular, is further developed in a later thought-provoking little book that offers a brain-based theory of human knowledge (*Second Nature: Brain Science and Human Knowledge*, 2006).

and functional–dynamic stances is as old as human thought, reflected in different Western and Eastern cultural traditions. In the history of psychology, the entailed dichotomy between the two stances is exposed in the tension between the functional versus structural world views, a tension that has given rise to a multitude of original and challenging ideas over the past century. Let us read a couple of paragraphs that concern these views as seen around the year 1900, before expressing a biased integration on the emergence of physiological objects, viewed from my position along the structural–programmatic functional–dynamic dimension.

At the turn of the twentieth century there was quite a split in academic psychology between the so-called structural (largely German) and functional (largely American) schools. Mary Whiton Calkins, in her presidential address to the American Psychological Association (1906),[111] described the distinguishing features of the two schools as follows:

> Structural psychology consists essentially in the teaching that the task of psychology is first, to analyze typical experiences until one reach irreducible elements, and second, to classify the ordinary sorts of complex experience according as one or another of these elements pre-dominates. The structural psychologist may, and does, supplement this analysis and classification by seeking for each experience or typical class of experiences a scientific explanation – that is, by seeking to link it with other facts, or groups of facts, whether psychic, physiological, or physical … [F]unctional psychologists … conceive the psychophysical organism as the basal fact of psychology, holding that the concern of psychology is with the relations of the functioning psychophysical self, the conscious body, to its environment … [F]unctional psychology includes the supplementary doctrine that consciousness is to be conceived and classified, not merely as relation in general, but as 'effective' or beneficial relation – in other words, as a function which has meaning or value.[112]

[111] Calkins (1863–1930) was the first woman president of the Association.
[112] Calkins (1906).

I concur with Calkins' position about the complementarity of both stances, the structural–programmatic and the functional–dynamic, although she is being diplomatic in this statement. The difference between structuralism and functionalism in the study of psychology *as a science* impacts on how things are understood and where research energy should be invested. Herbert Simon (1916–2001), one of the greatest minds in the twentieth century, demonstrates the effect by posing a didactically intended question: *How should the fact of many animals in the Arctic having white fur be explained?* Simon's answer is that we "usually explain this by saying that white is the best color for the Arctic environment, for white creatures escape detection more easily than do others,"[113] supplementing the explanation by a notion of natural selection, or some equivalent mechanism:

> *An important fact about this kind of explanation is that it demands an understanding mainly of the outer environment* [italics added]. Looking at our snowy surroundings, we can predict the predominant color of the creatures we are likely to encounter; we need know little about the biology of the creatures themselves, beyond the facts that they are often mutually hostile, use visual clues to guide their behavior, and are adaptive (through selection or some other mechanism).[114]

In the praxis of science as a basic intellectual endeavor (to be distinguished from applied aspects) the dictum of functionalism is very different from that of structuralism. The dictum – taken to the limit – implies that for psychology as a basic intellectual endeavor there is nothing to gain by looking into the brain of the individual, a conclusion that is similar to ideas expressed over the past one hundred years by many psychologists, from Wundt and Freud (depending which of his texts one chooses to cite), through Skinner to present-day voices calling to reject recent initiatives to "biologize" psychoanalysis.[115]

113 Simon (1996, pp. 7–8).
114 Ibid.
115 For example, Blass and Carmeli (2007), and references therein.

A similar difficulty surrounds the dimension of genetic-epigenetic impacts on development,[116] where the structural-programmatic stance is represented by claims about DNA being the "book of life" and the genome as a "genetic program" that defines the organism lock, stock, and barrel. In its extreme version this view calls for classifying the human subject according to the genes, giving rise to the present dominance of industrial biosciences. The functional–dynamic stance is represented by ideas of "top-down" or "downward causation," where the genome is understood as a kind of a sensory sheath that responds to environmental cues, and where the biological system is viewed as an *ensemble of potentials* from which the environment carves out a particular realization.

The birth of the functional school is often dated to John Dewey's seminal paper, published in Psychological Reviews (1896) "The Reflex Arc Concept in Psychology."[117] There, Dewey attacks structural psychologists who embrace a conceptual framework according to which the "sensory stimulus is one thing, the central activity, standing for the idea, is another thing, and the motor discharge, standing for the act proper, is a third."[118] Such undue generalization of the reflex arc framework to psychology, says Dewey,

> gives us one disjointed part of a process as if it were the whole. It gives us literally an arc, instead of the circuit; and not giving us the circuit of which it is an arc, does not enable us to place, to center, the arc.... The circle is a coordination, some of whose members have come into conflict with each other. It is the temporary disintegration and need of reconstitution which occasions, which affords the genesis of, the conscious distinction into sensory stimulus on one side and motor response on the other. The stimulus is that phase of the forming

[116] Denis Noble, a distinguished Oxford university physiologist, sharpens the arguments on this issue in an essay called *The Music of Life: Biology Beyond the Genome* (2006) and in a series of papers and recorded debates.

[117] Dewey (1896).

[118] Ibid., p. 358.

> coordination which represents the conditions which have to be met in bringing it to a successful issue; the response is that phase of one and the same forming coordination which gives the key to meeting these conditions, which serves as instrument in effecting the successful coordination. They are therefore strictly correlative and contemporaneous. *The stimulus is something to be discovered; to be made out* [italics added]; if the activity affords its own adequate stimulation, there is no stimulus save in the objective sense already referred to. As soon as it is adequately determined, then and then only is the response also complete. To attain either, means that the coordination has completed itself. *Moreover, it is the motor response which assists in discovering and constituting the stimulus* [italics added]. It is the holding of the movement at a certain stage which creates the sensation, which throws it into relief.[119]

The ideas expressed in this beautifully written text have kept on reverberating in neurophysiology and psychology until this day. In modern times Dewey's ideas are re-treated under different terminologies: for example, active sensing, perception–action cycle, predictive brain models, top–down sensory processing, and more.

One of the earliest psychological experiments that exposed – in a most convincing way – the meaning of Dewey's statements about the stimulus "to be discovered" assisted by the motor response, is the seminal Kitten Carousel project of Held and Hein.[120] They have arranged an experimental setting that assures simultaneous exposure of a pair of kittens to identical visual stimulation. The difference between the two was that one of them (the "active" kitten) was free to determine – by movement – the sensory experience. The other kitten simultaneously experienced that same sensory world passively, without being able to move. Although both experienced exactly the same visual world, only the active kitten – the one that "discovered" the sensory stimuli by moving and exploring – developed normal visual

[119] Ibid., p. 370.
[120] Held and Hein (1963).

functionality. Ideas that are similar to Dewey's vision on the stimulus being "discovered," "made out" by our behaviors, will be further discussed in the section on *Relations, Truth and Pathology*, and linked to relational objects in psychology and to the basal meaning of James's concept of Pragmatism as a process of truth-creation.

It is always the case in the history of science that when two extreme positions are available, repeated attempts to polarize them abound. The resulting debates are valuable, making readers fine-tune their own positions, which are invariably in between. I used to think that I fully identified with one and only one of the stances, the functional–dynamic. But while reading and preparing for the content of the present chapter, I found myself becoming more relaxed on these matters, being able to acknowledge that the position depends on the definition of the temporal scales involved. In the larger, slower cycle of life, interpretations in the spirit of the functional–dynamic stance are more appropriate, describing the struggle to adapt in a functional–dynamic Darwinian language. The potential outcome of a functional–dynamic process is a repertoire of adapted mechanisms, most of which are well-defined patterns of stimulus–response relations, to the description of which the structural–programmatic stance is suited. Hence, I now feel that the issue depends on whether one asks "what is there?" versus "how did it get to be there?" The answer to the former may benefit more from a structural–programmatic interpretation, whereas the answer to the latter *must* be phrased in functional–dynamic terms. This approach is intimately linked to the categorization of answers to the question "Why?," rooted in Aristotle's four causes (material, formal, efficient, and final)[121] and its modern Tinbergen's version, which considers the theory of evolution.[122]

121 Irwin (1998, pp. 419–20).

122 Nikolaas Tinbergen (1907–88), a Physiology & Medicine Nobel Prize laureate (shared with Konrad Lorenz and Karl von Frisch). In a 1963 paper he phrased the four questions facing the biology of behavior; see also Bateson and Laland (2013), a review of Tinbergen's four questions, 50 years later.

As for the aspect of "effectiveness" that was traditionally attributed to the functional but not to the structural stance, it is now readily accepted that programs may and should be conceived and classified as "effective" or "beneficial" in establishing meaningful relations with the environment. In this sense, the term functional-dynamic should be read as "dynamics that must give rise to functional relations," rather than as a term that denies the functional attribute from the structural-programmatic stance.

One central neurophysiological front in which the structural-programmatic versus functional-dynamic world views find expression, concerns the emergence of physiological objects, the subject matter to which the next section is dedicated.

The Emergence of Relational Objects

Most neurophysiologists contemplating processes underlying the emergence of objects would probably be tempted to think in terms of formation or change of neural representations, spatiotemporal patterns of neural activities. Underlying this tendency is the ubiquitous assumption of isomorphism between human behavior and patterns of electrical activity in the brain, an assumption that stands at the basis of all branches of modern neuroscience. I, of course, adopt this underlying assumption, being aware of no other reasonable alternative.

It is generally believed that behaviors are not interpretable to single action potentials generated by any one neuron; rather, behaviors – even the most simple imaginable – are interpreted in the language of physiology to groups of action potentials. These groups of action potentials may originate from a single neuron over time, or from populations of neurons that are active in synchronic or diachronic manners. The term *neural activity group* denotes such a set of action potentials to which a psychological object is interpreted; the term is general, not committed to the actual, physical nature of the underlying neural structure (which will be shortly discussed in a comment). Neural activity groups are believed to be formed and changed throughout life in a dynamic, history-dependent manner, conforming to evolution and environmental constraints.

Formation and change of neural activity groups – physiological objects – are often described using the terms "learning" and "adaptation," loaded words that carry many different meanings in the wider context of the life and social sciences. Throughout the text up until this point a generous use of the word adaptation was made, as if it is clear that it has only one accepted interpretation. This is not the case. In the discourse of genetics and evolution, adaptation denotes changes that in one way or another promote the functionality of a system or parts of a system. What geneticists call adaptation, neurophysiologists call learning, a word rarely used in genetics and evolution. The term adaptation is also ubiquitous in neurophysiological texts, although its meaning differs from that understood by geneticists and evolutionists. To clarify the issue, we turn to Klaus Krippendorff, a leading figure in the discipline of Cybernetics. Krippendorff offers to understand learning as a process of increased efficiency with which responses lead to desirable states, errors are avoided, or a portion of the world is controlled. This is not the same as adaptation, which he defines as implying changes in response to a changing environment, not necessarily of growing success.[123] While the general spirit of Krippendorff's definitions is useful for our purposes, they are overly value-laden (efficiency, desire, error, success); psychologists may provide us many examples of learned behaviors that are not desired or efficient, and hardly successful. Moreover, Krippendorff's definition is vague regarding the dynamics of relations between the

[123] Klaus Krippendorff's full definition of learning and adaptation in *A Dictionary of Cybernetics* (1986, unpublished report), is cited in: F. Heylighen, C. Joslyn, and V. Turchin (editors): *Principia Cybernetica Web* (Principia Cybernetica, Brussels), URL: http://cleamc11.vub.ac.be/learning.

subject and the environment. A modified definition is wanted that is less value-laden and more relational, a definition that relies on the concept of congruence as presented in Chapter 3.

I define *adaptation* as a process that *maintains congruent relations* with the environment amid changes in the latter, whereas learning is the process of *increasing congruence of relations* with the environment, whether the latter changes or not. In a pragmatist Jamesian language, adaptation is the process of adjusting an established truth about an object amid changes in object's features; learning, on the other hand, is the process of establishing new truth relations. For a system to become functional in the sense of establishing congruence with the environment, learning must take place; that is, a change in either the system or the environment or both. In other words, the "gastrulation" phenomenon of a developing conceptual nervous system – the formation of its initial rift – is learning, perhaps the most critical learning process in our life, a symmetry breaking that gives rise to the emergence of physiological objects.

The different approaches to the issue of learning in neurophysiology reflect the pushes and pulls along the spectrum extending from structural–programmatic to functional–dynamic stances. As a prototypical setting, consider the hungry baby: when facing the inevitable ambiguity of relations with the nourishing–retreating mother, he exhibits a repertoire of different behaviors (movements). As long as these behaviors of the baby do not bring and maintain the mother's breast close to him, his basic needs are not satisfied and he keeps on producing various movements. A set of movements, a behavior, that is followed by an approaching (or, at least not retreating) breast is supposed to relax him and be somehow imprinted so that in subsequent encounters with a similar situation the probability of producing the latter set of movements is increased.[124] As viewed

[124] Versions of the following arguments were previously published in contributions by Shahaf and Marom (2001), Marom and Eytan (2005), Braun and Marom (2009), Marom et al. (2009), and Marom (2010).

from the structural–programmatic stance, there is *a present state* (for instance, a breast afar or retreated from the baby) and *a desired state* (for instance, a feeding breast approaching or remaining within the baby's reach). What makes these two states relevant at a given point in time is the presence of *a global drive* – hunger, or some other need – linked to a physiological state in a manner that may be reasonably understood by physiologists. Such global drives constitute the interface, the boundary layer between the primitive psychological realm and the language of physiology. The behaviors are movements, *actions* that reflect the underlying structure of the relevant neural networks in the baby's brain, actions that might impact on the environment, possibly shifting it from one state to another. Any given behavior is produced by activation of a unique neural activity group that reflects a given configuration of instantaneous, effective relations among neurons in the baby's brain. If, following the movement, the breast remains afar or retreated from the baby, he keeps on exploring: that is, the neural activity group that gave rise to the said movement is more-or-less abandoned in favor of another group. In the most primitive version of the above picture, the exploration process is random while the reward is a function of the instantaneous distance between the present and the desired states, a measure of discontent. In more sophisticated realizations, the extent of reward is "computed" from the impact of recent behaviors on the progress toward a desired state, and the exploration is directed by an underlying rule that makes things more efficient. Interestingly, one such rule is the psychologically inspired association by simultaneity, Hebb's Rule, which has been discussed at length. As described here, the structural–programmatic proposition for the emergence of physiological objects is a *constructive* change in configurations of neural activity groups (that is, physiological objects), a process that is aroused by a physiological drive. The change is constructive in the sense of being guided, at least to some extent, by the distance from a desired state of relations with the environment.

This structural–programmatic neurophysiological picture of the learning process is appealing, congruent with well-established psychological learning theories and supported by quite an extensive physiological database. It is also numerically conceivable as testified in the vast literature of relevant computational analyses. Indeed, physiologists successfully identified different neural clusters that are located in the subcortex, the Φ area of the conceptual nervous system; the activities of these clusters are reasonably correlated with the occurrence of salient or desired environmental states that follow movements. Moreover, several of these neural clusters, when active, entail release of global neuromodulators onto the cortical (Ψ) area of the conceptual nervous system, modulators that are believed to somehow impact on the stability of recently successful neural activity group, hence establishing a physiological object.[125] Notably, the activity of these same Φ subcortical neurons, as well as their effects on the cortical Ψ neurons, are the critical sites of actions for major psychoactive substances, including psychiatric drugs.

Appealing as it may seem, the structural–programmatic approach raises many questions and awaits clarification and solidification. Proponents of this stance confront challenging issues, most of which concern the problem of implicitly assuming a priori knowledge in the brain. After all, we do know that the state space is unbounded, as indicated by measures at the levels of protein molecules and cells, neural networks, and the whole brain, as well as behavioral levels, entailing More Is Different and Less Is Not Simpler.[126] Where the number of

[125] Often mentioned in this context are neurons that cause release of the global neuromodulator dopamine, but other neurons that release different modulators (for example, serotonin, acetylcholine, noradrenalin) also show similar contingencies to the behavioral process of learning.

[126] The concept of state space immensity and its combinatorial consequences is lucidly presented by Walter M. Elsasser in his book *Reflections on a Theory of Organisms* (1987). For a review of state space immensity at the temporal domain in brain and behavior systems, see Marom (2010).

biological states is immense, the standards required for defining a discontent, let alone measuring and comparing it to some reference value, are difficult to conceive. What constitutes the scale of a system state? And within a given scale, what constitutes a unique state? What or who determines a state as desirable? Is there a metric, a standard of measurement that may be used to *physiologically* express a distance from a desired state without falling into the trap of linking "... the intentions of the experimenter (intentions to reward or punish) with good or bad behavior on the part of the animal"?[127] To handle these difficulties, structural-programmatic approaches must implement some degree of a priori knowledge, thus adopting Plato's stance as revealed in his description of Socrates' response to Meno's immortal question: "[H]ow will you enquire, Socrates, into that which you do not know? What will you put forth as the subject of enquiry? And if you find what you want, how will you ever know that this is the thing which you did not know?"[128] To which Socrates answers, after a long and polemic dialogue: "[The] soul must have always possessed this knowledge ... truth of all things always existed in the soul."[129] We do not learn new things, say Socrates, Plato, and modern proponents of the structural-programmatic approach to the problem of learning. We *re*member, *re*count.

The above requirement to assume *prior* knowledge is by no means unique to the brain sciences. Transcendent as we might wish it to be, the brain is part of the wider biological realm. And in biology, learning – as a process of increasing congruence of relations with the environment – is a ubiquitous phenomenon. How does the immune system learn to identify unforeseen pathogens? How does a colony of ants learn the routes from their nest to feeding sites with the information available to each single ant about the overall landscape being

[127] Guthrie (1946, p. 7) [Presidential address of the APA, Evanston, Illinois, 1945].
[128] *Meno*, by Plato, ca. 383 B.C., p. 46.
[129] Ibid., p. 55.

so scarce? How do bacteria learn to associate high temperature with lack of oxygen, given the small scale of the single bacterium, so small that temperature and oxygen gradients cannot be sensed along its head–tail axis? How can these phenomena be explained given the fact that in biological systems, unlike man-made machines, there is no designer nor a director, "someone who knows"; where we are not guaranteed scaling of the driving force with the gap between the present position and the desired one; where exploration is commanded by local variables that are independent of the global distance from a desired state, and rewards are often very delayed? What is the meaning of reward under these conditions? And finally, how can a system find a good enough solution to multiple interactional contexts, handling multitude of contradicting relations with the environment, without the exploration for one solution abolishing others? More generally phrased: what is the nature of mechanisms that enable reconfiguration of the immense number of entities involved in biological realizations of learning? The structural–programmatic stance does offer solutions to many aspects of these questions, provided that some extent of a priori knowledge is assumed, not so unreasonable an assumption given the evolutionary history of organisms.

I came to believe that the functional–dynamic approaches to the above learning related issues differ from the structural–programmatic approaches in matters of focus. Proponents of the functional–dynamic approach toward learning maintain that the values (good–bad, right–wrong, error, and so forth) implemented in constructive theories do not belong to the neural system itself, but rather to the larger complex that engulfs the environment, the system, and the observer. The alternative approach offered may collectively be referred to as the Drive Reduction framework,[130] according to which it is not necessary to assume a separate mechanism for the biological realization of an

[130] A term borrowed from Clark L. Hull (1884–1952), an influential American psychologist.

evaluative entity in distinction from the process of exploration for solutions. Rather, the behavioral concept of reward might be considered as a change (removal) in the drive underlying the exploration in the space of possible modes of a *network* response. A drive to explore that is removed when a desired state is achieved is an intention-less natural principle for adaptation to rich and unlabeled environment. The reduction of the drive is based on local cues and precludes the acquisition of new stimulus–response entailments. Sharpening of stimulus–response entailment, in turn, is achieved through a selection process.

Hence, the functional-dynamic interpretation to the emergence of internal physiological objects considers state-space immensity as a selection bed. This approach to learning classifies the operation of the brain as a Darwinian process,[131] similar to the processes taking place in the biological examples of the immune system, effective pattern formation in ant colonies, bacterial chemotaxis, and more. Biological learning thus viewed is a *population* phenomenon that involves exploration within immense configuration space, an exploration that relaxes when the population dynamics is congruent with that of the environment. A selective processes in which "... the *mode of genesis* of the worthy and the worthless seems the same,"[132] devoid of evaluative entities. Note that there is no need to assume an all-knowing observer to "tell" the neural system that a present configuration, a neural activity group, is incompatible with the demands of a behavioral constellation. Exploration within the unfathomable repertoire of possible Ψ neural activity groups is a natural consequence of activity-dependent changes of paths, occurring in practically every physiological time scale. Physiologists have observed and reported many forms of activity-dependent changes in neurons and their connections for almost a century. These processes are generally

131 Edelman (1987).
132 James (1950[1890], Volume 1, p. 552).

termed *plasticity* (short and long-term), *adaptation*, *accommodation*, *sensitization* and *de-sensitization*, *inactivation*, and so forth. As for discontent, it may take at least two forms: In the first, where the global drive mediated by the Φ subcortical system is not reduced by behavior, continuous activations that give rise to activity-dependent changes are entailed. In the second form, it is the mutual, ongoing, and reverberating activations within the cortical Ψ system that entail activity-dependent changes.

Wandering back and forth along the structural–programmatic functional-dynamic dimension, I do feel closer in heart to the latter. Yet it would be fair to say that, at least so far, the functional–dynamic framework has not provided formally satisfactory answers to the main problem of arriving at good enough congruence by means of unguided exploration within the immense state space. The general statement that convergence to congruent relations is theoretically plausible under such circumstances is a mathematical truism that may be demonstrated in well-controlled biological experiments. But the state of the art is far from being satisfactory, given the slow convergence rate that is often incompatible with real life constraints and the need to simultaneously cope with multiple contrastive relational contexts. This state of the art stands in a sharp contrast to the wealth of satisfactory formal treatments presented by proponents of the structural–programmatic approaches. Yet the latter should exercise much care to avoid the Tversky–Kahneman availability bias – that is, adhering to what is easily conceivable.[133] The fact that formal treatments of population-based Darwinian selection systems are far from being satisfactory, and difficult to conceive, does not imply that the impressive formal treatments of learning machines – designed by human and controlled by knowledgeable agents – are relevant to biology. This availability bias might have severe consequences within the context of biological reverse engineering and the dialectic nature

[133] Kahneman (2011).

of human relations with its environment, as already discussed in this book.[134]

To the extent that history of science may be used to predict the future, proponents of the functional–dynamic stance do have reasons to remain optimistic, as pointed out by Jerne:

> Looking back into the history of biology, it appears that wherever a phenomenon resembles learning, an instructive theory was first proposed to account for the underlying mechanisms. In every case, this was later replaced by a selective theory. Thus the species were thought to have developed by learning or by adaptation of individuals to the environment, until Darwin showed this to have been a selective process. Resistance of bacteria to antibacterial agents was thought to be acquired by adaptation, until Luria and Delbrück showed the mechanism to be a selective one. Adaptive enzymes were shown by Monod and his school to be inducible enzymes arising through the selection of pre-existing genes. Finally, antibody formation that was thought to be based on instruction by the antigen is now found to result from the selection of already existing patterns. It thus remains to be asked if learning by the central nervous system might not also be a selective process; i.e., perhaps learning is not learning either.[135]

One consequence of the above discussion on the formation of objects seems most relevant from the point of view of the physiology–psychoanalytic dialogue. Whichever way physiological objects emerge and are embodied, it is clear that the explorations involved in resolving the physiological discontent in early phases of interactive life are critical. Subsequent symmetry breaking processes have fewer degrees of freedom in the formation of neural activity groups because resolution of subsequent discontents must preserve the resolution of previous ones. One is tempted to project back to the idea of the "rift ... which never heals," as Freud called it,[136] the first

[134] See section on Reverse Engineering in Chapter 2, and opening remarks of Chapter 5; Vygotsky (1978); Kasparov (2010).
[135] Jerne (1967, p. 204).
[136] Freud (1938).

symmetry breaking and, being first, a split that dramatically impacts on later life splits, which – according to Ogden – are "built upon existing splits ... and do not involve creation of new ones."[137]

The level of abstraction exercised in the present essay is such that the physical nature of physiological objects – the neural activity groups – is beyond our scope. Nevertheless, it is proper, for the sake of psychologically educated readers, to briefly comment on this issue. Suppose that techniques are available that enable observation of every bit of activity in the subject's brain; how does a neural activity group, an object, "look like"? When a psychological process involves negotiating with the good-mother object, is there a "thing," a unique spatiotemporal form of activity that is the good-mother object? This is known as the question of representation schemes in neurophysiology. Much effort is invested in identifying the physical nature of neural activity groups, and we have learned a lot from experimental studies that focus on representation of relatively simple sensory and motor behavioral features: a unique tone, a bar of light, a particular face, arm movement to one place or another, gaze position, and so forth. The most challenging aspects of these studies concern neural activity groups in the subcortical and the Ψ cortical systems. It would be fair to summarize the results by saying that it is technically possible to identify spatiotemporal patterns of neural activity that are correlated with sensations or movements, but these patterns – especially when the Ψ cortical system is concerned – are neither unique nor stable over time. Representations are not unique in the sense of the same given behavior being correlated with different aspects of neural activities, often seemingly independent of each other. For instance, some neurophysiologists stress the precise timing and the specific identity of neurons as being the physical nature of neural activity group. Others might point to the overall activity of a group of neurons, regardless of which neuron is active and when. Moreover, no

[137] Ogden (1983).

one physical brain area may be identified as uniquely where the representation of any given behavioral object (sensory or motor) resides. Non-uniqueness of representations and their instability over time are reflections of the localization issue and its entailed conceptual difficulties, discussed at length in the beginning of this chapter. They also reflect the limits of reverse engineering in the context of More Is Different and Less Is Not Simpler, as discussed in Chapter 2. While the physical nature of neural activity groups, their stability, and their various embodiments, are important for those interested in applied neurophysiology (for example, brain stimulation as a symptomatic relief of neurological and psychiatric conditions), these issues are not germane to the physiology–psychoanalytic dialogue.

Relations Between Physiological Objects

Aspects of the relations between psychological objects, as outlined in Chapter 4, may be interpreted in the language of physiology, translated to forms of coupling among physiological objects, representations, or – as we have generally named them – neural activity groups. For this, however, we have to be satisfied with much less than the full psychoanalytic scope depicted in Chapter 4. This is the inevitable price paid for language relations and the entailed partial mappings; one would not know where to begin partitioning physiological objects to, for instance, "self," "good other," and "bad other." Having said this, the issue of the *form of relations* between objects, regardless of their attributions, is something that both the physiologist and the analytic psychologist might contemplate within the space of their dialogue. To the uninformed observer, the psychoanalytic arena might look as related to the content rather than the form of psychic processes. This is largely due to the clinically oriented origin of the theory and its heavy stress on subjective interpretation that is based on the content of the patient's words; the romantic view of a silent listener that says the right word at the right time. But psychoanalytic theory is much more than this; it always has been, certainly so as the discipline evolved and started focusing on *forms* of relations within abstract spaces of psychological existence. Perhaps the most significant achievement of the psychoanalytic theory in this respect is the acknowledgment of forms as carrying meaning, taken to the limit in the work of Winnicott, for whom – as pointed out by Ogden – meaning lies in the form as much as in the content.[138]

From the most elementary point of view, no matter what picture we have in mind for the physical nature of physiological objects – neural activity groups – the only means available for them to impact on each other or on external objects involves modulation of some form of energy transfer. Propagation of electrical action potentials, chemically transmitted via synaptic structures to other neurons or to muscles, is the form of energy transfer that is most ubiquitous in neural systems. Indeed, in instances where measurements are feasible, physiologists regularly observe stimulus-selective propagation of electrical activities among neural groups. Moreover, as one would expect in a reflexive, recurrent system, these activations are mutual in the sense that almost invariably some version of the activity is fed back to the neural group of origin. As discussed above, the quality of synaptic connectivity among neural activity groups may be either inhibitory or excitatory, and within each of these classes it can take a whole range of values, from the weakest to the strongest influence. The strengths of connections among neural groups are impacted by the short- and the long-term history of their activity, dictated by dynamic rules such as the association by simultaneity or variants thereof. But at this point, we are less interested in these mechanisms. What matters to us now is the overall picture of two objects (neural activity groups, to which we have interpreted the psychological concept of internal objects) that are dynamic in and by themselves, mutually coupled to each other to some extent, a coupling that is

[138] Ogden (1986, p. 204).

sensitive to the nature of their previous history over the short and the long terms.

In the world of abstract mathematical and physical constructs, this state of affairs goes under the name of coupled dynamic systems, a vibrant research field over the past twenty to thirty years. The actual mathematical formalisms involved are not our business; but lessons learned for the case of small (two or three) coupled systems are relevant to our dialogue, keeping in mind relational psychological objects and the intersubjective context.[139] It turns out that under a relatively wide range of conditions, such coupled dynamic systems tend to naturally form congruent relations. These relations are expressed in terms of instantaneous or delayed correlated activities, or as various repeated patterns of mutual activations. An external observer might classify the resulting interactions between the coupled objects using metaphoric terms such as predictive, suppressive, exciting, hierarchical, dominant, submissive relations, and so forth. But what actually pushes coupled dynamical systems to self-organize congruent relations with each other is the great and simple physical principle of minimization, in this case – minimization of interference with each other's dynamism. In the case of neural groups, activity-dependent changes in connectivity or modes of activity enable groups to evolve toward, find, or be attracted to spatiotemporal patterns that minimize mutual interference, patterns that are often named attractors, which might resume complex spatial and temporal architectures. In the transient phase – that is, during the relaxation toward these attractors – objects go through a physical exploration process, in which they might grow or contract, merge and split, be born and die. A large and most fertile body of biophysical analyses along these lines of attractor dynamics in networks of coupled neurons is found in the professional literature.

139 As recognized by Stolorow (1997) in a paper dedicated to the relevance of this physics framework to psychoanalysis.

It is important to acknowledge that such processes of group formation driven by relations with environmental constraints, abound and operate at various biological scales: in the formation of protein assemblies inside a single cell, through the emergence of spatiotemporal patterns in multicellular body tissues and populations of bacteria and yeast, the emergence of patterns in tracks of ant colonies, the enchanting concerts of fireflies flashing, all the way to human social interaction dynamics, to name but a few.[140] Thus the psychoanalytic idea of coupled dynamics of interacting internal objects that emerge due to constrained relations with a responsive environment, exploring for, and arriving at congruent relations, is not abstruse. It belongs to a large group of natural phenomena that are ubiquitously observed in different physiological systems. In the mathematical–physical field of coupled dynamical systems, this phenomenon is taken further by formulating coupling among many dynamic objects, analyses of feasibility and stability of coherent modes, and so forth. Much of the motivation underlying these abstractions comes from biology in general, and neurophysiology in particular.

Several of the vertices discussed so far – the language (or model) relations of Chapter 3, the psychological object relations theory of Chapter 4, and the dynamic nature of coupled groups of biological entities in general, and neurons in particular (the present Chapter 5) – share the same flavor of dialogic interactions between two rich entities that sample each other sparsely. There is one more vertex that is characterized by the same form of dialogic relations and validation by congruence, albeit between subjects and external objects as well as among subjects. It is the Jamesian concept of Pragmatism, already alluded to in several places. In the next section, Jamesian Pragmatism is offered as an agency through which a dialogue among the other

[140] For example, Gross and Sayama (Eds.), *Adaptive Networks, Theory, Models and Applications* (2009).

vertices may become instrumental as we contemplate object relations in health and disease.

Relations, Truth, and Pathology

Since Metaphysics of late without heirs to her fathers is gathered,
Here at the auctioneer's are 'things in themselves' to be sold.[141]

In a series of lectures delivered in Boston and New York during the winter of 1906–1907, William James (Figure 5.6) presented the idea of Pragmatism. James motivated his listeners and readers by offering Pragmatism as a method that mediates between intellectual abstraction and experiential connection with the actual world; between rationalism that gives rise to religious beliefs that are not based on facts, and empiricism that provides dry facts but denies humanism, whether religious or romantic.[142] But the scope of Pragmatism goes beyond methodology. It is about "what is meant by truth."[143] And it is here that the dialogical nature of psychological and physiological object relations resonates with Pragmatism. It is here, in the Jamesian acid test for meaning, where the genuineness of a dialogue between psychoanalysis and physiology rests.

James's main message in *Pragmatism*, especially in the sixth and the seventh lectures, is that the validity of an idea is not the static notion of correspondence between the idea and a truth that tags an object out there. Rather, *truth is the process of congruent relations* between the dynamics of the idea and those of the object. Truth *is made*, it *happens* to an idea and an object that are coupled to each other, rather than *being about* an idea or an object, echoing Dewey's concept of the stimulus to be discovered. One may interpret the Jamesian concept of truth of coupled idea–object, as *a process*, as "trueing." As such, it

141 *Goethe and Schiller's Xenions* (1915[1797]).
142 James (1907, Lecture 1, on The Present Dilemma in Philosophy, pp. 492–4).
143 Ibid., Lecture 2, on What Pragmatism Means, p. 515.

Figure 5.6 A portrait of William James, 1910.
William James (1910) by Ellen Emmet Rand. Oil on canvas; 138 × 106.1 cm. Harvard Art Museums/Fogg Museum, Harvard University Portrait Collection, Commissioned by the Department of Philosophy for the faculty room, 1910, H111. Photo: Imaging Department © President and Fellows of Harvard College.

means that truth depends on the internal dynamism of the individual (the subject) as much as on the dynamical features characterizing the object out there. This relational framework is not an easy conclusion to admit, as James writes:

> What hardens the heart of everyone I approach with … [this] view of truth … is that typical idol of the tribe, the notion of *the* Truth, conceived as the one answer, determinate and complete, to the one fixed enigma which the world is believed to propound. For popular tradition, it is all the better if the answer be oracular, so as itself to awaken wonder as an enigma of the second order, veiling rather than revealing what its profundities are supposed to contain. All the great single-word answers to the world's riddle, such as God, the One, Reason, Law, Spirit, Matter, Nature, Polarity, the Dialectic Process, the Idea, the Self, the Oversoul, draw the admiration that men have lavished on them from this oracular role. By amateurs in philosophy and professionals alike, the universe is represented as a queer sort of petrified sphinx whose appeal to man consists in a monotonous challenge to his divining powers. *The* Truth: what a perfect idol of the rationalistic mind! I read in an old letter – from a gifted friend who died too young – these words: "In everything, in science, art, morals and religion, there *must* be one system that is right and *every* other wrong." How characteristic of the enthusiasm of a certain stage of youth! At twenty-one we rise to such a challenge and expect to find the system. It never occurs to most of us even later that the question 'what is *the* truth?' is no real question (being irrelative to all conditions) and that the whole notion of *the* truth is an abstraction from the fact of truths in the plural, a mere useful summarizing phrase like *the* Latin Language or *the* Law.[144]

In contrast, he continues:

> What we [pragmatists] say about reality thus depends on the perspective into which we throw it. The *that* of it is its own; but the *what* depends on the *which*; and the which depends on *us*. Both the sensational and the relational parts of reality are dumb: they say absolutely nothing about themselves. We it is who have to speak for them.[145]

Much was said about the unfortunate choice of naming *Pragmatism* the rich Jamesian concept of truth process.[146] James himself wrote: "I

[144] Ibid., the opening of Lecture 7, on Pragmatism and Humanism, p. 591.
[145] Ibid., p. 594.
[146] Barzun (1983, p. 84).

do not like the name, but apparently it is too late to change it."[147] I propose that we use, for the purpose of the present discussion, a different, more indicative name for Jamesian Pragmatism: *relational dynamics*, denoting dialogic interactions in the large. Relational dynamics are reflected in a dialogue between coupled dynamic systems, or between languages as such, or between physiological objects, or between psychological objects or between subjects; or, indeed, between neurophysiology and psychoanalysis. Truth is the establishment of relational dynamics, validation by congruence, a reentry process that involves continuous interpretation–projection cycles, the nature of which is an inevitable product of earlier life with a subjective caregiver.

In the realm of mental relations, a truth process is a stream leading from one idea to the next, forming generative relations between inferences as depicted in the language relations of Chapter 3, or in the buildup of Bowlby's internal models (Chapter 4), or in state transitions of the dynamically coupled neural groups of the present Chapter 5. This whole structure of truth processes between objects within ourselves, truths that were initially set up by means of exhaustive exploratory negotiations with a constrained "mother reality" at the very early stages of our lives, is intensively committing: internal objects are sensitive to their roots, to those primary symmetry breaking events that preclude degrees of freedom. This is why one cannot simply point the attention of a subject to "a reality," asking him to see what one sees. For one's truth is incompatible with that of the other. Asking to change a given truth is no less than asking to change the relational dynamics between specific internal objects that are attached by strings of generative relations to a whole tree of other truths that happen at the same moment in time. I interpret the

[147] In the preface to *Pragmatism, A New Name for Some Old Ways of Thinking*, James (1907).

relations between psychological internal objects, as well as the transference relations between them and external objects, in the above light. When Ogden writes that we internalize objects and relations with them, an Ogdenian license may be taken to creatively read it[148] as internalization of a subject into a larger construct of truth dynamics; an internalization that unavoidably involves distortions entailed by the establishment of congruent relations with preexisting objects.

An internal object, psychological or physiological, is always in relational dynamics with other internal objects, as well as with external entities – subjects or objects – indirectly or directly. For the internal objects that are more directly related to external entities, the latter are essential, the fuelwood that keeps those internal objects "alive" or "engaged" in congruent relations. These internal objects that are directly engaged by the external world are critical determinants, psychologically and physiologically. They are the keyhole through which the environment samples the internal space and vice versa. One might imagine that under conditions where a significant external subject is missing or unintelligible (giving rise to "phantom" or inconsistent representation) a potentially severe impact on a whole network of internal object relations ensues. There is no void in these kinds of dynamics. Where congruent relations cannot be maintained, dynamics are diverted to alternative paths, commanded by the impassive principle of energy minimization, the resulting relational patterns of behavior being interpreted by an observer as forms of characteristic traits, normative or pathological.

In the extreme, dynamics within the inner space, between internal objects, become congruent to a degree rendering them practically insensitive to, or independent of the dynamics of external subjects or their representations. It sometimes happens in early adulthood or

148 Ogden (2012).

later in life, where congruence with external objects or subjects, individual or institutional, is severely challenged. The capacity of one to deal with the resulting discontents, dictated by early-life symmetry breaking, determines how intimately one flirts with the option of psychotic states of mind, that is – trueing within oneself, having congruent relational dynamics within, oblivious of the dynamics of external subjects and objects. As such, psychotic states are reflections of a default mode of inner space dynamism, the mode of action to which the conceptual nervous system seamlessly drawn in the absence of intelligible relations with the external world. Interestingly, when the cortical Ψ system is detached from subcortical Φ input, the former is attracted to ongoing, spontaneous dynamic modes of action,[149] which might activate existing objects otherwise reflecting congruent relations with external objects. This picture is supported by physiological observations indicating that ongoing activity of the cortical Ψ system, in the absence of sensory input, spontaneously and dynamically hops among representational objects.[150] A physiological condition that is reminiscent of this is the state of sleep, where the cortex feeds itself with its own activity, aided by interactions with the subcortex but detached from the periphery,[151] inviting reflection on dreams as unrestrained jumps between physiological objects, in the absence of external input.

Challenge for Relational Physiology

Let us close this chapter on physiological objects considering the methodological challenges entailed by the relational context in which the brain is embedded. Neuroscience is a relatively recent endeavor that evolved from and overshadows the traditional discipline of neurophysiology. Neuroscience is conceived in the public eye, and

[149] For example, Timofeev et al. (2000).
[150] Kenet et al. (2003).
[151] For example, Destexhe and Sejnowski (2009, pp. 973–6).

unfortunately also in the eyes of many practicing scientists, as if there are no limits to its explanatory power. This state of affairs should make us feel restless, because the hallmark of mature science is its ability to acknowledge its own limits, overcoming sentiments of omnipotence that characterize infantile stages of development. One may hope that future neuroscientific research will enable us to identify its boundaries, the limits of brain processes as valid explanations to behavior, expressing genuine acknowledgment and respect to the impacts of scale jumps. As stated in various places throughout this text, it would be very interesting to learn which behavioral phenomena reside outside the scope of physiology, at what level of structural organization the understanding of behavior becomes intellectually autonomous of its microscopic realization. Even further, what characterizes the larger class of systems that enable complex organism-like behavior – neurons being only one exemplar?

At present, too many neuroscientists delude themselves in believing that all that is required are measuring tools that allow one to look closer and closer, to find "the" machinery, "the" particle, "the" coordinates of complex behavior inside the brain; as if nothing resides outside, in the relational dynamics between entities, or between the brain, objects and subjects in the environment. One reason for the adherence to such a naive course is its implementability within standard scientific paradigms. Stated differently, there is currently no known alternative, more appropriate conceptual framework to scientifically handle relational contexts. The study of structural–programmatic aspects of a given system under well-defined and largely static environmental constraints is a natural extension of traditional paradigms in engineering and physical sciences. Within these paradigms we feel comfortable; we know how to optimize the design of experiments, how to perturb or displace the system and what to measure, how to build mathematical models of the system, and how to do the right statistics to optimize the models. From the very early stages of our science education we are instructed to define control parameters, or independent variables, and how to carefully record order parameters or dependent variables that characterize the observed state of the system. Prevailing physiological and laboratory-based psychological inquiries implement this tradition by exercising maximal control on the presentation of stimuli. Indeed, when a stimulus – be it an object or a human subject – becomes unstable over the experimental session or (Heaven forbid!) sensitive to the state of the observed system, our observation is often deemed unsatisfactory. The "ideal observer" stance of traditional analysts in clinical settings is an expression of this framework, reflecting the science envy of the founder of psychoanalysis.

But the dominance of relational contexts in evolutionary and ontogenic history of humans, as advanced throughout this chapter, calls for reexamining this tradition. There is something very unnatural, one dare say pathological, in establishing relational dynamics with a static, "dead" object. It is true that a subject may actively explore various features of static stimuli, but any given stimulus feature in these standard designs remains the same regardless of the subject's behavior. Hence, no feedback between the subject's actions and stimulus evolution is established; the dynamics is nonrelational. To uncover relational, functional–dynamic aspects of systems that are embedded in interactive environments – to expose the impacts of discontent, the resulting symmetry breaking, the entailed relational objects and their adaptive potential – new experimental concepts are called for. These should reflect acknowledgment that the individual brain is a cluster of cells, not much more; all the "rest" – all things that are psychologically meaningful – are "out there," in the relations of the embodied brain with the environment. The wanted experimental designs should allow the observed system to change its driving forces based on interactions with meaningful, dynamical, and responsive objects. This is not something that we know how to characterize. Unlike the framework of structural–programmatic approach, there is no comprehensive theory that caters to measurements and their interpretations under such conditions. The inability to separate the system's dynamics from those of its environment stands at the basis of our limits in the study of brain and its relations to behavior. Vygotsky saw it, almost one hundred years ago. "The search for method" he said, "becomes one of the most important problems of the entire enterprise of understanding the uniquely human forms of psychological activity. In this case, the method is simultaneously prerequisite and product, the tool and the result of the study."[152] In its broader sense, these problematics go far beyond physiological stimuli; they touch upon what relational psychologists have tried to tell us over the past forty years on the developing mind, when we – physiologists – care to listen.

[152] Vygotsky (1978, p. 65).

6 Sempiterna Temptatio

Physiological discourse was dominated for almost two millennia by the conceptions of Hippocrates (c. 460–370 B.C.) and Galen (A.D. 130–200) on the human body and its systems. Health and disease were explained in structural terms as reflecting a "balance," or lack of balance, between four bodily fluids: blood, yellow bile, black bile, and phlegm. Likewise, human personality: people were classified as excessively sanguine, choleric, melancholic, or phlegmatic, based on the dominant fluid, determined by *internal* structural factors. The idea of diseases as consequences of interactions between physiological systems and *external* agents gained popularity in the late sixteenth century, much influenced by the work of Paracelsus, enmeshing ancient Hermeticism with alchemy, magic, and Christianity.[1] For Paracelsus, the physiology of a human being cannot be understood in separation from its physical and spiritual surroundings; a forerunner of Dewey's functionalism, Jamesian pragmatism, Vygotsky's historical–cultural dialectic psychology, and the more recent approaches of relational and intersubjective psychology, all arguing for dynamics of humans and their environments as inseparable.

But the appeal of the structuralism of Hippocrates and Galen remained dominant throughout. Especially its manifestation in terms of explaining the higher by the lower, "treated forever as a case of 'nothing but' – nothing but something else of a quite inferior sort,"[2]

[1] Webster (1982).
[2] James (1907, p. 493).

buried deep inside the body of the individual, awaiting discovery by analyzing "discrete structures further and further down in the scale of things, whole *raison d'être* is to be found entirely within ourselves."[3] We still hear specialists talking about internal "chemical imbalance" as a cause of mental illness, be it excessive or reduced activity of dopamine, serotonin, norepinephrine, or glutamate, and – further down the scale of things – on this or that group of genes that determines our personality and its normal or pathological manifestations. These reducing forces are tempting; they always have been. Whether it is God or Gene, phlegm or dopamine, we need the notion of "... *The* truth, conceived as the one answer, determinate and complete, to the one fixed enigma which the world is believed to propound."[4]

What is this enigma – *truth* – that we are so troubled by? Truth of what? Had we consulted a specialist in philosophy, we would have been offered as many answers to this question as there are philosophical writings. Being a physiologist with marginal sensitivity to metaphysical finesse, I tend to shy away from formal philosophical literature, preferring the more accessible language of reflective scientists. Among the latter, it is the answer offered by a distinguished geneticist, Richard C. Lewontin, that resonates well with my personal biases. In one of the chapters of a monograph, "Biology as Ideology: the Doctrine of DNA,"[5] Lewontin presents a view according to which the enigma that troubles us, and to which we desperately seek simple structural-programmatic answers, is no less than the enigma of inequality. Being chosen by God or his representatives to bestow to your sons (less so to your daughters) the right to belong to the upper class, having a blue fluid running in your veins and bequeathed to your sons such that "blood will tell," or if you happen to have those good genes that are passed on in the family – these are

[3] Bridgman (1927, p. 93).
[4] James (1907, p. 591).
[5] Lewontin (1991, pp. 19–37).

all different ways to justify inherent inequality and hierarchical society. How else can we explain to ourselves why this particular man, or woman, or child suffers so, and the other does not? How else can we explain the facts of poverty and wealth running in families? And in the past 300 years, says Lewontin, since the political revolutions that swept out the old aristocratic order that justified itself by appeal to God, church, or blood, we have to deal with the immense gap between the unavoidable observation of inequality in societies that proudly raise the flag of *Liberté, Egalité, Fraternité*. This is where biology takes over, becoming instrumental by offering inherited innate differences as an answer to the enigma; replacing one capital G with another.

The alternatives of functional approaches to the enigma, those that imply relational dynamics with the environment, are far from satisfactory. They are doomed to fail in the short term because they are always less definitive, they are too general and not obviously applicable, they are romantic and abstract, and their proponents are willing to accept the *impossible* as valid no less than the *possible*. Yet these alternatives are important in being, poling biological determinism, and as such need to be actively protected; this essay is my contribution – limited as it may be – to active protection against biological determinism.

A most touching expression of the inherent tension between the reducing structural–programmatic and the relational functional–dynamic approaches is found in the great novel of Marguerite Yourcenar *The Abyss*, describing the life and death of Zeno, a physician–philosopher-alchemist, a collage of Paracelsus, da Vinci, Copernicus, and many others, having a type of mind that stands:

> halfway between the subversive dynamism of the alchemists and the mechanistic philosophy which is to prevail in the immediate future, between hermetic beliefs which postulate a God immanent

> in all things and an atheism barely avowed … a type of mind not uncommon to the age, but which may be said to have crossed the Renaissance almost subterraneously, remaining closer both to the Middle Ages and to our own times.[6]

Here are Zeno's words, admirably humble, acknowledging the ethereal temptation to succumb to a reductive, naive scientism, as to the humanistic duty of opposing it:

> *Sempiterna Temptatio*, … I often say that nothing in the world, if not a divine order, or a strange whim of matter to outdo itself, explains why I strive each day to think a little more clearly than the evening before.… Never shall I cease to marvel that this flesh sustained by its vertebrate, this trunk joined to the head by isthmus of the neck and disposing its members symmetrically about itself, contains and perhaps even produces a mind which makes use of my eyes in order to see and my movements in order to touch … I know this mind's limitations, and know that it will not have time to go further, or the strength, if by chance enough time be accorded to it. But this mind *is*, and in this moment, it is the *One who Is*. I know that it makes mistakes, goes astray, and often wrongly interprets the lessons which the world doles out to it; but I know, too, that it has within itself the capacity to recognize and sometimes to rectify its own errors. I have traversed at least one part of this sphere where we are; I have studied the fecundation of plants and the point at which metals fuse; I have observed the stars and have examined the inside of bodies. From this brand that I lift here I can deduce a concept of weight, and from these flames the concept of warmth. What I do not know, I know full well that I do not know, and I envy those who will eventually know more; but I know also that, exactly like me, they will be obliged to measure, weigh, deduce, and then mistrust the deductions so produced; they will have to make allowance for the part which is true in any falsehood, and likewise reckon the eternal admixture of falsity in truth.[7]

[6] Yourcenar, 1976[1968], pp. 364–6.
[7] Ibid., pp. 122–3.

Determinism has always been difficult to pole, more so in the Middle Ages, where people paid with their lives for questioning, as Zeno of Bruges did. Rather than fear and confusion that tempted humans to reduce into naive determinism in the Dark Ages, modern times exploit our narcissistic tendencies at this service, where science and scientists, judged and ranked by the extravagance of their statements, go down a path leading to enslavement by technology, the price of which is ever growing.

I wished Freud and James to meet again, to rectify a failure to dialogue that I fantasized to have happened in that 1909 short walk to the Worcester railway station. I wanted to hear them discussing, debating the beauty and hazards involved in negotiating psychoanalysis and physiology, the means to resist the temptation of resorting to the coziness of naive determinism, the structural–programmatic stance. So much I wished them to meet that I yielded to romantic ideas of searching for evidence of a meeting in Europe during the last year of James's life. James, in fact, did sail to Europe during the spring and summer of 1910, a last visit to the continent he loved. The trip was meant to enable James and his wife, Alice, to nurse his melancholic brother Henry, who had lived and written in Rye, South East England, since 1897 until his death in 1916. William James, suffering from severe cardiac symptoms, continued from Rye to Bad Nauheim in Germany to rest, later joined by Henry and Alice. Alice had "two invalids on her hands," says Richardson, citing a sentence in her diary: "William cannot walk and Henry cannot smile."[8] William James died on August 26, on his way back to America.

Apparently, I am not the only one with dreams of parental rejoining.[9] They probably did not meet; or, if they did, that meeting left no

[8] Richardson (2007, p. 518).

[9] "There are two or three clues that they may have also met again, when James, it has been alleged, secretly slipped into Vienna for a consultation with Freud in March of 1910, just a few months before James himself died" (Taylor, 1999).

discernible intellectual impact. But we are here, endowed with public trust, responsible for the education of our students to develop their own intellectual integrity. When it comes to negotiations between psychology and physiology, the burden seems heavier than ever and needs to be handled with much care. In this long letter I have contemplated a space for a relational dialogue between psychoanalysis and physiology, a reverential dialogue that respects the scale horizons of two beautiful disciplines that touch the things that are most important to each and every one of us, body and mind.

This essay emerged from discontent, and working through it brought a significant relief to me; something relaxed. I hope it will be useful to others, even if only a few. I return now – at least for a while – to physiology, where my heart and reason belong, as I am yours,

S.M. October 2013

Bibliography

Abeles, M. (1991). *Corticonics: Neural Circuits of the Cerebral Cortex*. Cambridge University Press.

Adrian, E.D. (1926). The impulses produced by sensory nerve endings: Part 1. *The Journal of Physiology*, 61, 49–72.

Adrian, E.D., and Zotterman, Y. (1926a). The impulses produced by sensory nerve-endings: Part 2. The response of a single end-organ. *The Journal of Physiology*, 61, 151–171.

(1926b). The impulses produced by sensory nerve endings: Part 3. Impulses set up by touch and pressure. *The Journal of Physiology*, 61, 465–483.

Aiello, L.C., and Dunbar, R.I. (1993). Neocortex size, group size, and the evolution of language. *Current Anthropology*, 34(2), 184–193.

Amaral, D. (2000). The Anatomical Organization of the Central Nervous System. In E.R. Kandel, J.H. Schwartz, and T.M. Jessell (Eds.), *Principles of Neural Science*. McGraw-Hill.

Anderson, P.W. (1972). More is different. *Science*, 177, 393–396.

(2001). More Is Different – One More Time. In N.P. Ong, and R.N. Bhatt (Eds.), *More is Different: Fifty Years of Condensed Matter Physics*. Princeton University Press.

Andrews, B.W., Sontag, E.D., and Iglasias, P.A. (2008). An approximate internal model principle: Applications to nonlinear models of biological systems. *Proceedings of the 17th IFAC World Congress*, 15873–15878.

Aron, L. (1996). *A Meeting of Minds: Mutuality in Psychoanalysis*. The Analytic Press.

Atlan, H. (1989). Natural Complexity and Self-Creation of Meaning. In *Mind over Matter*. Israel Academy of Sciences and Humanities.

(1993[1986]). *Enlightenment to Enlightenment: Intercritique of Science and Myth*. State University of New York Press.

Bain, A. (1874). *Mind and Body: the Theories of Their Relation*. D. Appelton & Company.
Barzun, J. (1983). *A Stroll With James*. Harper & Row.
Bassingthwaighte, J.B., Liebovitch, L.S., and West, B.J. (1994). *Fractal Physiology*. Oxford University Press.
Bateson, P., and Laland, K.N. (2013). Tinbergen's four questions: an appreciation and an update. *Trends in Ecology & Evolution*, 28, 712–718.
Beale, L.S. (1864). Indications of the paths taken by the nerve-currents as they traverse the caudate nerve-cells of the spinal cord and encephalon. *Proceedings of the Royal Society of London*, 13, 386–392.
Bennett, M.R. (1999). The early history of the synapse: from Plato to Sherrington. *Brain Research Bulletin*, 50, 95–118.
Bethe, H.A. (1965). High energy physics. *Science*, 147, 1551–1552.
Blass, R.B., and Carmeli, Z. (2007). The case against neuropsychoanalysis: On fallacies underlying psychoanalysis' latest scientific trend and its negative impact on psychoanalytic discourse. *The International Journal of Psychoanalysis*, 88, 19–40.
Borges, J.R. (1975). Exactitude in Science. In N.T. de Giovanni (Trans.), *A Universal History of Infamy*. Penguin Books.
(1998). Funes, his Memory. In A. Hurley (Trans.). *Collected Fictions*. Penguin Books.
Boring, E.G. (1950[1929]). *A History of Experimental Psychology*. Appleton-Century-Crofts.
Bowlby, J. (1973). *Separation: Anxiety and Anger* (Attachment and Loss, Volume 2). The Hogarth Press & the Institute of Psycho-Analysis.
(1988). *A Secure Base*. Basic Books.
Braitenberg, V. (1977[1973]). *On the Texture of Brains: An Introduction to Neuroanatomy for the Cybernetically Minded*. Springer-Verlag.
Braun, E., and Marom, S. (2009). Learning Without Error. In G. Hon, J. Schickore, and F. Steinle (Eds.), *Going Amiss In Experimental Research*, Volume 267, 49–54. Springer.
(2014). Universality, complexity and the praxis of biology: two case studies. *Studies in History and Philosophy of Science C*. (in-press).
Bridgman, P.W. (1927). *The Logic of Modern Physics*. Macmillan Publishing.
Brothers, L. (1997). *Friday's Footprint: How Society Shapes the Human Mind*. Oxford University Press.
Bullmore, E., and Sporns, O. (2012). The economy of brain network organization. *Nature Reviews Neuroscience*, 13, 336–349.

Buonomano, D.V., and Merzenich, M.M. (1998). Cortical plasticity: from synapses to maps. *Annual review of neuroscience*, 21, 149–186.

Bush, E.C., and Allman, J.M. (2003). The scaling of white matter to gray matter in cerebellum and neocortex. *Brain, Behavior and Evolution*, 61, 1–5.

Butler, A.B., and Hodos, W. (2005). *Comparative Vertebrate Neuroanatomy: Evolution and Adaptation*. Wiley & Sons.

Calkins, M.W. (1906). A reconciliation between structural and functional psychology. *Psychological Review*, 13, 61–81.

Carhart-Harris, R.L., and Friston, K.J. (2010). The default-mode, ego-functions and free-energy: a neurobiological account of Freudian ideas. *Brain*, 133, 1265–1283.

Carmeli, Z., and Blass, R. (2013). The case against neuroplastic analysis: A further illustration of the irrelevance of neuroscience to psychoanalysis through a critique of Doidge's "The Brain that Changes Itself" *The International Journal of Psychoanalysis*,94, 391–410.

Constantinople, C.M., and Bruno, R.M. (2013). Deep cortical layers are activated directly by thalamus. *Science*, 340, 1591–1594.

Cook, I., and Lipkin, M. (1972). *Cellular Neurophysiology: A Source Book*. Holt, Rinehart and Winston.

Damasio, H., Grabowski, T., Frank, R., Galaburda, A.M., and Damasio, A.R. (1994). The return of Phineas Gage: clues about the brain from the skull of a famous patient. *Science*, 264, 1102–1105.

Dennett, D.C. (1995). Cognitive science as reverse engineering: several meanings of "top-down" and "bottom-up". *Studies in Logic and the Foundations of Mathematics*, 134, 679–689.

Destexhe, A., and Sejnowski, T.J. (2009). Sleep and Sleep States: Thalamic Regulation. In L.H. Squire (Ed.), *Encyclopedia of Neuroscience*. Elsevier.

Dewey, J. (1896). The reflex arc concept in psychology. *Psychological Review*, 3, 357–370.

Dunbar, R.I.M. (2003). The social brain: mind, language, and society in evolutionary perspective. *Annual Review of Anthropology*, 32, 163–181.

Eccles, J.C. (1989). *Evolution of the Brain: Creation of the Self*. Routledge.

Edelman, G.M. (1987). *Neural Darwinism: The Theory of Neuronal Group Selection*. Basic Books.

(1992). *Bright Air, Brilliant Fire: on the Matter of the Mind*. Basic books.

Edelson, M. (1984). *Hypothesis and Evidence in Psychoanalysis*. University of Chicago Press.

Elsasser, W.M. (1998[1987]). *Reflections on a Theory of Organisms*. The Johns Hopkins University Press.

Fairbairn, W.R.D. (1944). Endopsychic structure considered in terms of object-relationships. *The International Journal of Psychoanalysis*, 25, 70–92.

Fehr, E., Bernhard, H., and Rockenbach, B. (2008). Egalitarianism in young children. *Nature*, 454, 1079–1083.

Feynman, R. (1985[1965]). *The Character of Physical Law*. The M.I.T. Press.

Finger, S. (1994). *Origins of Neuroscience*. Oxford University Press.

Finlay, B.L., Darlington, R.B., and Nicastro, N. (2001). Developmental structure in brain evolution. *Behavioral and Brain Sciences*, 24, 263–278.

Flugel, J.C. (1934). *A Hundred Years of Psychology: 1833–1933*. The Macmillan company.

Foley, P.C., and Lee, R.A. (1991). Ecology and energetics of encephalization in hominid evolution. *Philosophical Transactions of the Royal Society (B)*, 334, 223–232.

Francis, B.A., and Wonham, W.M (1975). The internal model principle for linear multivariable regulators. *Applied Mathematics & Optimization*, 2, 170–194.

Freud, S. (1895). Project for a Scientific Psychology (1950[1895]). In J. Strachey, editor, *The Standard Edition of the Complete Psychological Works of Sigmund Freud, Volume I (1886–1899): Pre-Psycho-Analytic Publications and Unpublished Drafts*. Vintage, the Hogarth Press, and the Institute of Psycho-Analysis, 2001[1959].

(1910). "Wild" Psycho-analysis. In J. Strachey, editor, *The Standard Edition of the Complete Psychological Works of Sigmund Freud, Volume XI (1910): Five Lectures on Psycho-Analysis, Leonardo da Vinci and Other Works*. Vintage, the Hogarth Press, and the Institute of Psycho-Analysis, 2001[1959].

(1917). Mourning and Melancholia. In J. Strachey, editor, *The Standard Edition of the Complete Psychological Works of Sigmund Freud, Volume XIV (1914–1916): On the History of the Psycho-Analytic Movement, Papers on Metapsychology and Other Works*. Vintage, the Hogarth Press, and the Institute of Psycho-Analysis, 2001[1959].

(1920). *A General Introduction to Psychoanalysis*. Horace Liveright.

(1920a). Beyond the Pleasure Principle. In J. Strachey, editor, *The Standard Edition of the Complete Psychological Works of Sigmund Freud, Volume XVIII (1920–1922): Beyond the Pleasure Principle, Group Psychology and Other Works*. Vintage, the Hogarth Press, and the Institute of Psycho-Analysis, 2001[1959].

(1925). An Autobiographical Study. In J. Strachey, editor, *The Standard Edition of the Complete Psychological Works of Sigmund Freud, Volume XX (1925–1926): An Autobiographical Study, Inhibitions, Symptoms and Anxiety, Lay Analysis and Other Works*. Vintage, the Hogarth Press, and the Institute of Psycho-Analysis, 2001[1959].

(1927). Fetishism. In J. Strachey, editor, *The Standard Edition of the Complete Psychological Works of Sigmund Freud, Volume XXI (1927–1931): The Future of an Illusion, Civilization and its Discontents, and Other Works*. Vintage, the Hogarth Press, and the Institute of Psycho-Analysis, 2001[1959].

(1938). Splitting of the Ego in the Process of Defence. In J. Strachey, editor, *The Standard Edition of the Complete Psychological Works of Sigmund Freud, Volume XXIII (1937–1939): Moses and Monotheism, An Outline of Psycho-Analysis and Other Works*. Vintage, the Hogarth Press, and the Institute of Psycho-Analysis, 2001[1959].

(1954) *The Origins of Psycho-Analysis: Letters to Wilhelm Fliess, Drafts and Notes: 1887–1902 by Sigmund Freud*. Basic Books.

(1995[1938]). *The Basic Writings of Sigmund Freud*. The Modern Library.

Freud, S., and Jones, E. (1993). *The Complete Correspondence of Sigmund Freud and Ernest Jones 1908–1939*. Edited by R. A. Paskauskas. The Belknap Press of Harvard University Press.

Friston, K. (2009). The free-energy principle: a rough guide to the brain? *Trends in Cognitive Science*, 13, 293–301.

Futagi, Y., Toribe, Y., and Suzuki, Y. (2012). The grasp reflex and Moro reflex in infants: hierarchy of primitive reflex responses. *International Journal of Pediatrics*, Volume 2012 (Article ID: 191562).

Gay, P. (1998). *Freud: A Life For Our Time*. W. W. Norton.

Gifford-Gonzalez, D. (2007). On beasts in breasts. Another reading of women, wildness and danger at *Çatalhöyük*. *Archaeological Dialogues*, 14, 91–111.

von Goethe, J.W., and Schiller, F. (1915[1797]). *Goethe and Schiller's Xenions. Selected and translated by P. Carus*. Open court Publishing Company (a BiblioLife reproduction).

Gramsci, A. (1971). *Antonio Gramsci (1891–1937), Selections from the Prison Notebooks of Antonio Gramsci*. International Publishers.

Gross, T., and Sayama, H. (2009). *Adaptive Networks, Theory, Models and Applications*. Springer.

Guthrie, E.R. (1946). Psychological facts and psychological theory. *Psychological Bulletin*, 43, 1–20.

Havel, I.M. (1996). Scale dimensions in nature. *International Journal of General System*, 24, 295–324.

Hebb, D.O. (1949). *The Organization of Behavior: a Neuropsychological Theory*. John Wiley & Sons.

(1955). Drives and the CNS (Conceptual Nervous System). *Psychological Review*, 62, 243–254.

Held, R., Hein, A. (1963). Movement-produced stimulation in the development of visually guided behavior. *Journal of Comperative and Physiological Psychology*, 56, 872–876.

Herculano-Houzel, S. (2009). The human brain in numbers: a linearly scaled-up primate brain. *Frontiers in Human Neuroscience*, 3.

Heylighen, F. (2001). The Science of Self-Organization and Adaptivity. *The Encyclopedia of Life Support Systems*, 5:253–280.

Heylighen, F., Joslyn, C., Turchin, V. (1994). *Principia Cybernetica Web*. [URL: http://pespmc1.vub.ac.be/].

Hill, R.A., and Dunbar, R.I.M. (2003). Social network size in humans. *Human Nature*, 14, 53–72.

Hopfield, J., and Tank, D. W. (1986). Computing with neural circuits: a model. *Science*, 233, 625–633.

Howarth, C., Gleeson, P, and Attwell, D. (2012). Updated energy budgets for neural computation in the neocortex and cerebellum. *Journal of Cerebral Blood Flow Metabolism*, 32, 1222–1232.

Hull, C. (1943). *Principles of Behavior*. New York: Appleton-Century-Crofts.

Irwin, T.H. (1998). Aristotle. In *Routledge Encyclopedia of Philosophy*, Volume 1, Edward Craig (General Editor). Routledge.

Isaacs, S. (1948). The nature and function of phantasy. *The International Journal of Psychoanalysis*, 29, 73–97.

James, W. (1950[1890]). *The Principles of Psychology* (in two volumes). Dover Publications.

(1902). The Varieties of Religious Experience. In *William James Writings 1902–1910*. Literary Classics of the United States, 1987.

(1907). Pragmatism, a New Name for Some Old Ways of Thinking. In *William James Writings 1902–1910*. Literary Classics of the United States, 1987.

(1909). The Meaning of Truth. In *William James Writings 1902–1910*. Literary Classics of the United States, 1987.

(1920). *The Letters of William James*, H. James (editor), in two volumes. A public domain book, Atlantic Monthly Press.

Jensen, K., Hare, B., Call, J., and Tomasello, M. (2006). What's in it for me? self-regard precludes altruism and spite in chimpanzees. *Proceedings of the Royal Society (B)*, 273, 1013–1021.

Jerne, N. (1967). Antibodies and Learning: Selection versus Instruction, In G.C. Quarton, T.H. Melenchuk, and F.O. Schmitt (Eds.), *The Neurosciences: a Study Program*, 200–205. Rockefeller University Press.

Jones, E. (1955). *The Life and Work of Sigmund Freud, Volume II: Years of Maturity 1901–1919*. Basic Books.

Jung, C.G. (1972). The Mother Archetype. In *Four Archetypes*. Routledge & Kegan Paul.

Kahneman, D. (2011). *Thinking Fast and Slow*. Penguin Books.

Kandel, E.R. (1998). A new intellectual framework for psychiatry. *The American Journal of Psychiatry*, 155, 457–469.

(1999). Biology and the Future of Psychoanalysis: A New Intellectual Framework for Psychiatry Revisited. *The American Journal of Psychiatry*, 156, 505–524.

Kandel, E.R, Schwartz, J.H., and Jessell, T.M. (2000). *Principles of Neural Science*, Fourth Edition. McGraw-Hill.

Kaplan-Solms, K., and Solms, M. (2000). *Clinical Studies in Neuro-Psychoanalysis: Introduction to a Depth Neuropsychology*. Karnac.

Karlsson, G. (2010[2004]). *Psychoanalysis in a New Light*. Cambridge University Press.

Kasparov, G. (2010). The Chess Master and the Computer. *The New York Review of Books*, 57.

Kenet, T., Bibitchkov, D., Tsodyks, M., Grinvald, A., and Arieli, A. (2003). Spontaneously emerging cortical representations of visual attributes. *Nature*, 425, 954–956.

Kernberg, O.F. (1987). An ego psychology-object relations theory approach to the transference. *The Psychoanalytic Quarterly*, 56, 197–221.

Klein, M. (1975). Notes on Some Schizoid Mechanisms. In *Envy and Gratitude & Other Works 1946–1963*. Hogarth Press and the Institute of Psycho-Analysis.

Klerman, G.L. (1990). The psychiatric patient's right to effective treatment: implications of Osheroff v. Chestnut Lodge. *The American Journal of Psychiatry*, 147, 409–418.

(1991). The Osheroff debate: finale. *The American Journal of Psychiatry*, 148, 387–390.

Kobayashi, H., and Kohshima, S. (2001). Unique morphology of the human eye and its adaptive meaning: comparative studies on external morphology of the primate eye. *Journal of Human Evolution*, 40, 419–435.

Krishnan, A., Giuliani, A., and Tomita, M. (2007). Indeterminacy of reverse engineering of gene regulatory networks: the curse of gene elasticity. *PLoS One*, 2(6), e562.

Kumar, A., Vlachos, I., Aertsen, A., and Boucsein, C. (2013). Challenges of understanding brain function by selective modulation of neuronal subpopulations. *Trends in Neurosciences*, 10, 579–586.

Lagunoff, D. (2002). A Polish, Jewish scientist in 19th-century Prussia. *Science*, 298, 2331.

Laufer, E. (ed.) (2012). *The Psychoanalytic Review Special Issue. On the Frontiers of Psychoanalysis and Neuroscience: Essays in Honor of Eric R. Kandel*. Guilford Press.

Lazebnik, Y. (2004). Can a biologist fix a radio? – or, what I learned while studying apoptosis. *Biochemistry* (Moscow) 69, 1403–1406.

LeDoux, J. (1996). *The Emotional Brain*. Simon and Schuster.

(2000). Emotion circuits in the brain. *Annual Review of Neuroscience*, 23, 155–184.

Lee, P.N., Kumburegamab, S., Marlowa, H.Q., Martindale, M.Q., Wikramanayake, A.H. (2007). Asymmetric developmental potential along the animal-vegetal axis in the anthozoan cnidarian, Nematostella vectensis, is mediated by Dishevelled. *Developmental Biology*, 310, 169–186.

Lent, R., Azevedo, F.A., Andrade-Moraes, C.H., and Pinto, A.V. (2012). How many neurons do you have? Some dogmas of quantitative neuroscience under revision. *European Journal of Neuroscience*, 35, 1–9.

Lewin, R. and Foley, R.A. (2004). *Principles of Human Evolution*. (2nd edition). Blackwell Publishing.

Lewontin, R.C. (1991). *Biology as Ideology: The Doctrine of DNA*. Harper Perennial.

Mach, E. (1914). *The Analysis of Sensations and the Relations of the Physical to the Psychical*. Translated from the 1st German edition

by C.M. Williams; revised and supplemented from the 5th German edition by Sydney Waterlow. Published by Open Court Publishing Company.
Marom, S. (2010). Neural timescales or lack thereof. *Progress in neurobiology*, 90, 16–28, 2010.
Marom, S., and Eytan, D. (2005). Learning in ex-vivo developing networks of cortical neurons. *Progress in Brain Research*, 147, 189–199.
Marom, S., and Shahaf, S. (2002). Development, learning and memory in large random networks of cortical neurons: lessons beyond anatomy. *Quarterly Reviews of Biophysics*, 35, 63–87.
Marom, S., Meir, R., Braun, E., Gal, A., Kermany, E., and Eytan, D. (2009). On the precarious path of reverse neuro-engineering. *Frontiers in Computational Neuroscience*, 3.
Matsuzawa, T. (2013). Evolution of the brain and social behavior in chimpanzees. *Current Opinion in Neurobiology*, 23, 443–449.
McGuire, W. (1974). *The Freud-Jung Letters: The Correspondence Between Sigmund Freud and CG Jung*. Princeton University Press.
Miller, A., Alston, R., and Corsellis, J. (1980). Variation with age in the volumes of grey and white matter in the cerebral hemispheres of man: measurements with an image analyser. *Neuropathology and applied neurobiology*, 6, 119–132.
Minerbi, A., Kahana, R., Goldfeld, L., Kaufman, M., Marom, S., and Ziv, N.E. (2009). Long-term relationships between synaptic tenacity, synaptic remodeling, and network activity. *PLoS Biology*, 7(6), e1000136.
Mitchell, S.A. (1993). *Hope and Dread in Psychoanalysis*. Basic Books.
(2000). *Relationality: From Attachment to Intersubjectivity*. The Analytic Press.
Myowa-Yamakoshi, M., Scola, C., and Hirata, S. (2012). Humans and chimpanzees attend differently to goal-directed actions. *Nature Communications*, 3 (Article number: 693).
Noble, D. (2006). *The Music of Life: Biology Beyond Genes*. Oxford University Press.
(2008). Genes and causation. *Philosophical Transactions of the Royal Society (A)*, 366, 3001–3015.
Ogden, T.H. (1983). The concept of internal object relations. *The International Journal of Psychoanalysis*, 64, 227–241.
(1986). *The Matrix of the Mind*. Jason Aronson Inc.
(2012). *Creative Readings, Essays on Seminal Analytic Works*. Rutledge.

Panksepp, J. (1998). *Affective Neuroscience: The Foundations of Human and Animal Emotions*. Oxford University Press.

Panksepp, J., and Biven, L. (2012). *The Archaeology of Mind: Neuroevolutionary Origins of Human Emotions*. (Series of Interpersonal Neurobiology), W.W. Norton.

Plato. *Meno*. B. Jowett (Trans.), a Public Domain Book (Kindle edition).

Richardson, R.D. (2007). *William James: In the Maelstrom of American Modernism*. Mariner Books.

Rosen, R. (1978). *Fundamentals of Measurement and Representation of Natural Systems*. North-Holland New York.

(1985). *Anticipatory Systems: Philosophical, Mathematical, and Methodological Foundations*. Pergamon Press.

(1991). *Life Itself: a Comprehensive Inquiry Into the Nature, Origin, and Fabrication of Life*. Columbia University Press.

Rosenzweig, S. (1992). *Freud, Jung, and Hall the King-Maker: the Historic Expedition to America (1909), with G. Stanley Hall as host and William James as guest*. Hogrefe & Huber Publishers.

Segal, H. (1975). *Introduction to the Work of Melanie Klein*. Hogarth Press.

Shahaf, G., and Marom, S. (2001). Learning in networks of cortical neurons. *The Journal of Neuroscience*, 21, 8782–8788.

Simon, H.A. (1996). *The Sciences of the Artificial*. The M.I.T. Press.

Skinner, B.F. (1938). *The Behavior of Organisms: an Experimental Analysis*. Appleton-Century.

(1950). Are theories of learning necessary? *Psychological Review*, 57, 193–216.

Solms, M., and Turnbull, O.H. (2011). What is neuropsychoanalysis? *Neuropsychoanalysis*, 13(2), 133–145.

Sontag, E.D. (2003). Adaptation and regulation with signal detection implies internal model. *Systems & Control Letters*, 50, 119–126.

Spencer, H. (2011[1885]). *The Principles of Psychology*. In *The Works of Herbert Spencer*, a Kindle edition.

Stolorow, R.D. (1997). Dynamic, Dyadic, Intersubjective Systems: An Evolving Paradigm for Psychoanalysis. *Psychoanalytic Psychology*, 14:337–346.

Stolorow, R.D., and Atwood, G.E. (1992). *Context of Being: The Intersubjective Foundations of Psychological Life*. The Analytic Press.

Stone, A.A. (1990). Law, science, and psychiatric malpractice: a response to Klerman's indictment of psychoanalytic psychiatry. *The American Journal of Psychiatry*, 147, 419–427.

Swanson, L.W. (1995). Mapping the human brain: past, present, and future. *Trends in Neurosciences*, 18, 471–474.

Szymborska, W. (1976). Utopia. S. Baranczak, and C. Cavanagh (Trans.), in: *Poems New and Collected 1957–1977*. Harcourt.

Talvitie, V., and Ihanus, J. (2011). On neuropsychoanalytic metaphysics. *The International Journal of Psychoanalysis*, 92, 1583–1601.

Taylor, E. (1999). William James and Sigmund Freud: the future of psychology belongs to your work. *Psychological Science*, 10, 465–469.

Timofeev, I, Grenier, F., Bazhenov, M., Sejnowski, T.J., and Steriade, M. (2000). Origin of slow cortical oscillations in deafferented cortical slabs. *Cerebral Cortex*, 10, 1185–1199.

Tinbergen, N. (1963). On aims and methods of Ethology. *Zeitschrift für Tierpsychologie*, 20, 410–433.

Tobias, P.V. (1981). The emergence of man in Africa and beyond. *Philosophical Transactions of the Royal Society (B)*, 292, 43–56.

Tomasello, M. (1999). *The Cultural Origins of Human Cognition*. Harvard University Press.

(2014). *A Natural History of Human Thinking*. Harvard University Press.

Tomasello, M., Hare, B., Lehmann, H., and Call, J. (2007). Reliance on head versus eyes in the gaze following of great apes and human infants: the cooperative eye hypothesis. *Journal of Human Evolution*, 52, 314–320.

Van Essen, D.C. (1997). A tension-based theory of morphogenesis and compact wiring in the central nervous system. *Nature*, 385, 313–318.

Vlachos, I., Zaytsev, Y.V., Spreizer, S., Aertsen, A., and Kumar, A. (2013). Neural system prediction and identification challenge. *Frontiers in Neuroinformatics*, 7.

Vygotsky, L.S. (1978). *Mind in Society: The Development of Higher Psychological Processes*. Harvard University Press.

Wagner, S., Sagiv, N., and Yarom, Y. (2001). Gaba-induced current and circadian regulation of chloride in neurons of the rat suprachiasmatic nucleus. *The Journal of Physiology*, 537, 853–869.

Webster, C. (1982). *From Paracelsus to Newton: Magic and the Making of Modern Science*. Cambridge University Press.

Weisskopf, V.F. (1965). A defence. *Science*, 147, 1552–1554.

Wennekamp, S., Mesecke, S., Nédélec, F., and Hiiragi, T. (2013). A self-organization framework for symmetry breaking in the mammalian embryo. *Nature Reviews Molecular Cell Biology*, 14, 452–459.

Wilkes, A.L., and Wade, N.J. (1997). Bain on neural networks. *Brain and Cognition*, 33, 295–305.

Winnicott, D.W. (1960). The theory of the parent-infant relationship. *The International Journal of Psychoanalysis*, 41, 585–595.

Wundt, W. (1912). *An Introduction To Psychology*. George Allen & Unwin.

Xerri, C. (2012). Plasticity of cortical maps: multiple triggers for adaptive reorganization following brain damage and spinal cord injury. *The Neuroscientist*, 18, 133–148.

Yourcenar, M. (1976[1968]). *The Abyss (L'Oeuvre au Noir)*. Farrar, Straus and Giroux, Gallimard.

Zhang, K., and Sejnowski, T.J. (2000). A universal scaling law between gray matter and white matter of cerebral cortex. *Proceedings of the National Academy of Sciences*, 97, 5621–5626.

Zilles, K., Armstrong, E., Schleicher, A., and Kretschmann, H.J. (1988). The human pattern of gyrification in the cerebral cortex. *Anatomy and Embryology*, 179, 173–179.

Index

Lightning Source UK Ltd.
Milton Keynes UK
UKHW021438231019
352120UK00014B/339/P

9 781107 101180